it even happens in "GOOD" schools

it even happens in "GOOD" schools

responding to cultural diversity
in today's classrooms

Festus E. Obiakor

foreword by Bob Algozzine
afterword by Robert Rueda

CORWIN PRESS, INC.
A Sage Publications Company
Thousand Oaks, California

For information:

Corwin Press, Inc.
A Sage Publications Company
2455 Teller Road
Thousand Oaks, California 91320
CORWIN   E-mail: order@corwinpress.com
PRESS

Sage Publications Ltd.
6 Bonhill Street
London EC2A 4PU
United Kingdom

Sage Publications India Pvt. Ltd.
M-32 Market
Greater Kailash I
New Delhi 110 048 India

Printed in the United States of America

Library of Congress Cataloging-in-Publication Data

Obiakor, Festus E.
  It even happens in "good" schools: Responding to cultural diversity in today's classrooms / by Festus E. Obiakor.
    p. cm.
  Includes bibliographical references and index.
    ISBN 0-7619-7795-3 (c : alk. paper) — ISBN 0-7619-7796-1 (p : alk. paper)
    1. Classroom management—United States—Case studies. 2. Teacher- student relationships—United States—Case studies. 3. School environment— United States— Case studies. 4. Multicultural education—United States— Case studies.   I. Title.
  LB3013 .O25 2000
  371.102'3—dc21   2001000299

This book is printed on acid-free paper.

01   02   03   04   05   06   07   7   6   5   4   3   2   1

Acquiring Editor: Robb Clouse
Corwin Editorial Assistant: Kylee Liegl
Production Editor: Diane S. Foster
Editorial Assistant: Candice Crosetti
Typesetter/Designer: Denyse Dunn
Indexer: Molly Hall
Cover Designer: Michelle Lee

Contents

Foreword

The experience of being called names and treated poorly because of where your parents come from or the perception others have of your heritage is an old one. Many move to the "land of opportunity," to "the other side of the tracks," to "the better part of town," and to "a good school" to overcome criticism, discrimination, and mistreatment and to build a better life for themselves and their children. They hope to reclaim the dignity they are entitled to as human beings and as citizens of a country where dreams and ideals of individualism, equal opportunity, nationalism, and success prevail and are the basis for fundamental human rights and continuing social responsibilities. Too often, it just doesn't work out that way. Too often, diversity that should be celebrated is the source of disparaging remarks, continuing intolerance, and disenfranchising treatment—even on the right side of the tracks, even on the right side of town, even in the "good" schools.

Dealing with diversity is certainly not a new concept in America. Multiple voices have been part of the country's educational system for a very long time. For example, in the 1850s, over half of New York City's residents were immigrants. Administrators and teachers in every period of educational history have had to think about both the challenge and the certainty of dealing with people from different cultures in schools. At the beginning of the 20th century, when compulsory attendance laws forced children from all ranges of society, not just the privileged, to go to school, special education programs cropped up in large cities to address the growing need for services for "exceptional children," children at the margins, many of whom came from rich, albeit nonmajority, cultures. Today, American public schools arguably serve a more diverse population than ever before in history. Race and ethnicity, social class, gender, national origin, native language, and disability contribute to the rich and diverse cultures that many children bring to school today. The challenge that remains is exploring, entertaining, and enriching what schools can do to promote educational experiences that are fully capable of serving diverse students and their families well.

It Even Happens in "Good" Schools: Responding to Cultural Diversity in Today's Classrooms provides perspectives of great value in this quest. Crossing "cases" with critical practices related to identification, assessment, categorization, placement, and instruction, Dr. Obiakor carries the reader on a journey that challenges, informs, and enlightens. Arguing that truly good schools are places where the potential of *all* students is maximized, he consistently illustrates the importance of addressing diversity in doing this. By the stories he tells and the questions he asks, he points out that progress is slow-moving and that quality, equity, and fair, appropriate treatment are, more often than not, very hard to find, even in "good" schools. Arguing that all schools must respond to pleas for excellence and quality, he shows us that these will not happen without concern for diversity as well. The book is punctuated with observations, solutions, and key points that should be invaluable in efforts to reform, restructure, and improve schools by translating research, resources, and rhetoric into fundamentally sound, "culturally responsive" professional practice.

In a very readable style, Dr. Obiakor presents challenging and practical information reflecting multiple perspectives, points of view, and philosophies. The lessons to be learned from the stories he tells are abundant, varied, and important; consider a few examples:

- Diverse student experiences belong in the classroom and enrich what is going on there.

- What a student is called, where he or she is placed, and how he or she is taught speak volumes about how much we value him or her.
- Perceptions affect assessment and instruction.
- Lack of language should never be misconstrued as lack of intelligence.
- A common goal of teachers must be to minimize negative consequences of testing.
- Behaviors (good and bad) of teachers have far-reaching consequences.
- Learning environments should be manipulated to meet the needs of all students.
- Good teaching is the engine behind good schools.

It is difficult to argue with Dr. Obiakor's ultimate conclusion: A good school is defined by how it addresses diversity. If his vision is embraced, misidentification, discrimination, and mistreatment will be reduced, and the benefits of having a truly good school, a dream school, will be realized by *all* learners, *all* teachers, *all* parents, and *all* communities.

BOB ALGOZZINE
University of North Carolina at Charlotte

Preface

It Even Happens in "Good" Schools: Responding to Cultural Diversity in Today's Classrooms is an important book that I have been trying to write for many years. The "it" in this title is a pregnant construct that specifically refers to the inadequate identification, assessment, categorization, and placement that are ingredients of poor teaching. Globally, the "it" may refer to subtle and obvious discrimination, bigotry, or xenophobia. In consonance with the book's theme, the adjective *good* qualifies any of our nation's schools. In spite of our pride and prejudice, all schools have some goodness or potential goodness in them. The goal is to make every one of them good using all available resources.

As I look back at the 1954 *Brown v. Board of Education of Topeka, Kansas* case and our latest drive toward full inclusion in schools, I am left to wonder if our rhetoric matches our action. I am forced to ask, "Is this an old wine in a new bottle or a new wine in an old bottle?" Educators are faced with either blindly maintaining the traditional culture of the teaching profession or iconoclastically destroying the foundations of the teaching profession. These two extremes are wrong. I am reminded of the African fable of "two knives," in which the sharp knife does not have a handle, and the knife with a handle is not sharp. From my perspective, we need to be progressive traditionalists who believe in maintaining the traditional culture of the profession, yet believe in making it progressive and modern. So, it makes sense that we strive to have a sharp knife with a solid handle!

Our debates on good teaching have been a little retrogressive and disingenuous. I believe we do not need teachers just because they are White or Black, or because they made high scores in standardized tests. We need good teachers who are progressive thinkers—such teachers believe in "quality with a heart." In my conversations with scholars, educators, college students, high school students, middle school students, and elementary school students, it seems to me that we all agree on what good teachers do. We all also agree on what good schools mean. As a result, I become very surprised and disappointed when goodness in schools is politicized by even those whom we think will understand. No child likes a school with mean, insensitive, and inconsiderate teachers! Not long ago, I asked my children why they liked a particular school over another, and they collectively noted that in the good school, people smile, teachers care, and the principal greets students. This statement demonstrates what Dr. Thomas Lovitt (1977) wrote in his book *In Spite of My Resistance. . . . I've Learned From Children.* How many teachers talk with or listen to their students? And how many parents talk with or listen to their children? The "good" school phenomenon has become puritanical. We act as if we are divorced from our children and youth. It actually reminds me of someone taking a gun and shooting himself or herself in the foot. To a large measure, truly good teachers are not afraid of doing the right things (e.g., assessing and teaching appropriately). It's almost a taboo to have fun while teaching—*funness* is today misconstrued as *weakness.* In fact, any difference is viewed as a deficit. How can the teaching-learning process respond to the unique needs of students who act, talk, learn, and look differently when any difference is viewed as a deficit?

We are now in the 21st century, a century that is witnessing tremendous shifts in paradigms and powers, especially in the education of our children and youth. In more ways than one, education has been called on to improve individual and collective growth. This call for improvement has rightly or wrongly led to the rat race for school reforms, some of which have been focused on accountability. Although the call for accountability has yielded slight gains in standardized norm-referenced test scores, it is doubtful that it has produced well-balanced growth in individual students. We have prescribed and used narrow, unidimensional perspectives to educate diverse students who are culturally, racially, linguistically, and socioeconomically different. We have also defined good schools from perfectionist perspectives—there are feelings that "good" schools are located in "good" neighborhoods or in rich communities that mirror cultural, linguistic, and socioeconomic homogeneity. From my perspective, these views are not only wrong but also phony because they fail to deal with demographic and societal changes and realities.

This book responds to the critical question "What is a good school?" I believe a good school is a learning community that maximizes the potential of *all* its students, whether they are Anglo Americans, African Americans, Hispanic Americans, Asian Americans, or Native Americans. A school cannot be a good school when some of its students are misidentified, misassessed, mislabeled, miscategorized, misplaced, and misinstructed. I argue that a good school is a school with good teachers who have the courage to teach with real pedagogical power. We cannot and should not define good schools only from the perspective of their students' high test scores. A good school should holistically educate the total child—academically, socially, emotionally, culturally, and globally. We want to produce critical thinkers, divergent thinkers, and problem solvers in our good schools. We cannot afford to have culturally myopic, narrow-minded teachers who cannot build on the strengths and energies that students bring to the classroom.

In this book, I thoroughly discuss the good school phenomenon using pertinent cases that expose real experiences of real people. My experiences have been helpful in documenting these cases. I believe that in every personal experience there are multiple educational lessons, and we must learn from them! Good teachers are good students who consistently broaden their horizons—these teachers know who they are, learn the facts when they are in doubt, change their thinking, use resource persons, build self-concepts, teach with divergent techniques, make the right choices, and continue to learn. This book goes beyond tradition and introduces readers to basic ingredients of good schools where good teachers teach with enthusiasm.

As it appears, this book is thematically divided to address educational phases. Although these phases may appear independent, they are mutually inclusive. Good teachers have the power to shift their paradigms as they decipher visible inconsistencies and errors in these phases—most important, they have the power to do something about them. As students interact with peers, as students interact with teachers, and as teachers interact with parents, collaboration, consultation, and cooperation must transcend all relationships. We must believe that "it takes a responsible village to raise a responsible child." The self, family, school, community, and government must work together to educate students for life. The whole village must be at work as students are appropriately identified, assessed, labeled, included, and instructed. As a consequence, throughout this book I advocate a "no-one-size-fits-all" technique. I believe that all good techniques must respond to intraindividual and interindividual differences in students!

In this book, many innovative ideas are espoused. They mean a lot to me! I want them to mean a lot to all readers (teachers, parents, administrators, professors, graduate and undergraduate students, researchers, consultants, community leaders, and experts). Although I do not believe this book is a panacea for all our school problems, I believe it offers unlimited multidimensional strategies for tackling these problems.

Acknowledgments

As always, this book would be impossible without the love and support of my wife, Pauline, and our children, Charles, Gina, and Kristen. I continue to cherish the wisdom and advice of my friends and well-wishers—they have meant a lot to me. I especially thank Dr. Bob Algozzine and Dr. Robert

Rueda for writing the Foreword and Afterword of this book.
Finally, my sincere thanks go to Cathy Mae Nelson for typ-
ing the original manuscript and for making some editorial
suggestions.

About the Author

Festus E. Obiakor, Ph.D., is Professor in the Department of Exceptional Education, University of Wisconsin–Milwaukee. He is a teacher, scholar, and consultant with a national and international reputation. He has served as Distinguished Visiting Professor/Scholar at Frostburg State University, Hendrix College, Indiana University of Pennsylvania, the University of Georgia, Eastern Illinois University, Abilene Christian University, West Virginia University, Hampton University, Marquette University, Illinois State University, and Brigham Young University. He is the author or coauthor of more than 100 publications, including books, articles, and essays, and he has conducted workshops and presented papers at local, state, regional, national, and international levels.

To my late father,
Chief Charles O. Obiakor,
Agbako I of Obodoukwu, Nigeria

and

To all *good* teachers who
shift their paradigms and
powers to maximize the
fullest potential of *all* students.

**CORWIN
PRESS**

The Corwin Press logo—a raven striding across an open book—represents the happy union of courage and learning. We are a professional-level publisher of books and journals for K–12 educators, and we are committed to creating and providing resources that embody these qualities. Corwin's motto is "Success for All Learners."

1

Redefining "Good" Schools

Conclusion

We need good schools for all of our nation's children. Interestingly, the "good" school phenomenon has overtaken our sense of obligation or decency. We seem to have forgotten that good schools are environments that should respond to the differences in styles, energies, and strengths that students bring to classrooms. In good schools, students from different cultural, racial, linguistic, and socio-economic backgrounds are expected to maximize their fullest potential. In such schools, teachers are expected to teach, test, reteach, and retest students in multidimensional, unprejudicial ways. Such schools are expected to prepare students to be productive citizens of the society (Grossman, 1998; Ladson-Billings, 1994; Obiakor, 1994). In addition, such schools are supposed to be havens for good students, good parents, good teachers, good principals, and good school district administrators. Ironically, the good school phenomenon has led to a deceptive self-aggrandizement in students, parents, teachers, and administrators. What really is a "good" school?

This chapter answers the question and sets the stage for other chapters in this book. Throughout the book, pertinent cases are used to discuss the "good" school phenomenon and why we need truly good teachers and good schools for *all* students.

To redefine good schools, we must view "culture" as an uncontroversial issue that increases the goodness and quality of schools (Banks, 1999; Ladson-Billings, 1994; Obiakor, 1994). The pervasive theme in this book is that good schools are environments where all students maximize their fullest potential. I argue that in this new millennium good schools must address demographic and cultural shifts in powers and paradigms. These shifts inevitably demand that good teachers and good schools utilize new methods of identification, assessment, categorization, placement, and instruction to deal with the multidimensional needs of all students, in spite of their cultural, racial, and socioeconomic backgrounds. The logical extension is that when identification and assessment are performed properly by teachers they lead to appropriate categories, placements, and instructions (Grossman, 1998; Obiakor, 1994, 1999a, 1999b, 1999c; Obiakor, Schwenn, & Rotatori, 1999).

In redefining good schools, I use cases to explicate classroom realities because cases are popular in educational research and pedagogy. Many scholars and educators (e.g., Grossman, 1998; Kohl, 1988; Ladson-Billings, 1994; Obiakor, 1994; Paley, 2000; Palmer, 1998; Smith, 1999; West, 1993) have used cases to tell their stories. Pedagogically, students learn from stories because they relate to real-life experiences. In fact, experiences can be instructional whether they are "good" or "bad." In many communities, especially in minority communities, oral tradition (in the form of storytelling) has been consistently honored as a respectable form of transmitting historical information. According to Denzin (1995), cases "create experiences that embody cultural meaning, and cultural understandings that operate in the 'real' world" (p. 8). They are experiences and self-stories that make up important events in people's lives. Denzin explained that they open "a parallax of discordant voices, visions, and feelings" and "yield to a ca-cophony of voices demanding to be heard (and seen)" (p. 18). Colbert, Trimble, and Desberg (1996) concluded that cases provide powerful means of learning through experiences. In their words, "Cases represent an interesting paradox in that they are deeply personal, evolving out of an individual's experiences, yet objective, in that they are designed to train teachers to function effectively in dealing with some of the most difficult problems they may face" (p. xiii).

Considering current demographic changes in today's schools, interest in books like this one has increased and will continue to increase. I believe that good schools must be defined from the perspective of their willingness to create innovative ways of providing quality education for all students. Our tra-ditional methods of solving problems in today's classrooms have not been very successful. Even teachers with "good hearts" do not know how to respond because of cultural in-competence, poor preparation, and unpreparation. Rigidity does not define good schools because it is frequently retrogres-sive. From my perspective, quality must go hand-in-glove with a heart, and how we manipulate classroom environ-ments affects the "goodness" of classrooms. My research and experience in the fields of general and special education have helped me redefine good schools. While interacting with teachers and professionals through the years, I documented lots of cases in supposed good classrooms and schools. In more specific terms, my documentations have been based on my roles as student, teacher, student-teaching supervisor, teacher-observer, classroom-based researcher, teacher-educator, parent, and consultant. These experiences have helped me see not just with my eyes but also with my "head" and "heart." I am convinced that because teachers teach from their personal experiences or cultural frames of reference, some of their methods may be misconstrued as racism even when they honestly believe they are helping students. However, the fact remains that they cannot teach what they do not know. As a consequence, continuous education is definitely key!

(recomend 1-wh)

The "Good" School Phenomenon

Good schools must be where teachers have the courage to teach. In such schools, educational practitioners must believe in "quality with a heart" because quality without a heart is like a house without a roof. It is not surprising that some politicians are almost at war with teachers, and vice versa. Equally not surprising is the fact that some teachers are at war with parents, and vice versa. Sadly, the construct *quality* has become the political watchword for school reformers. Palmer (1998) observed,

> In our rush to reform education, we have forgotten a simple truth: reform will never be achieved by reviewing appropriations, restructuring schools, rewriting curricula, and revising tests if we continue to demean and dishearten the human resource called the teacher on whom so much depends. Teachers must be better compensated, freed from bureaucratic harassment, given a role in academic governance, and provided with the best possible methods and materials. But none of that will transform education if we fail to cherish and challenge the human heart that is the source of good teaching. (p. 3)

Teachers must put their hearts and souls into what they do. It is not enough for teachers to be knowledgeable, and it is not even enough that they teach in "good" schools. Furthermore, it is not enough to know that these "good" schools are located in "good" neighborhoods where middle- to upper-class parents live. This myth of socioeconomic dissonance has defined our conception of good schools. Consider the recent school shootings and killings in many of our suburban and rural schools that have been consistently labeled "good" schools. Should "good" schools not be where students are safe and where good teaching and learning take place? According to Palmer (1998), "teaching and learning are critical to our individual and collective survival and to the quality of our lives. The pace of change has us snarled in complexities, confusions,

and conflicts that will diminish us, or do us in, if we do not en-
large our capacity to teach and to learn" (p. 3). Can the capaci-
ties to teach and learn be expanded in environments where
students' stressors are frequently swept under the rug as long
as they maintain good grades or good scores on standardized norm-referenced tests? Lovitt (2000); Obiakor, Darling,
and Ford (2000); and Obiakor, Mehring, and Schwenn (1997)
concluded that students' stressors impinge upon teaching
and learning and that teachers and practitioners with good
hearts minimize such stressors.

The good school phenomenon is alive and well! The critical
question is this: Can a school be a good school without a good
principal or administrator? There is a tendency to view schools
as *good* even when they have very *bad* principals or administrators. The ignorance of principals and school district administrators affects the "goodness" of their schools and teachers.
Because good schools must respond to societal realities, the
perceptions of principals and administrators about students,
especially those who are minorities and at risk, should be
taken seriously. Baer (1991) emphasized,

We need to understand who these kids are. They have
potential; however, they don't know it. They need what
we all have to offer, but they won't believe it. In a way,
they may want to fail because there is a kind of comfort in
that. After all, it's what they know best. Failure is a rest-
ful place to be. Nobody bothers them much because they
can't be expected to give or participate. . . . The crucial
point to remember is that in spite of all these obstacles,
these kids have all the potential that other kids have.
(p. 25)

It appears that changing perceptions about people, events,
and situations is painstaking. But for schools to be "good,"
teachers, principals, and administrators must leave their comfort zones. Consider Case 1, the case of Regina, the principal.

Case 1

Regina was a White female who headed a "good" elementary school located in a "good" neighborhood. She had the reputation of being a "good" principal. She went on a vacation to Guatemala in Central America. When asked about how she enjoyed her trip, she expressed frustration, saying that she did not enjoy it because the Guatemalan people failed to speak English. According to her, "If we should go there to spend our money, they must speak our English language."

At first glance, Regina sounds like a proud American. However, another look at the big picture exposes a close-minded person who has total disregard for other people's cultural and linguistic differences. The following pertinent questions should stimulate our thinking on our definition of a good school:

1. How can Regina work with students from culturally and linguistically diverse backgrounds or the parents of such students in her school?
2. How can Regina work with faculty or staff who come from culturally and linguistically diverse backgrounds?
3. Because the laws now require Regina to be involved in the special education program of her students, what will her input be in the placement of a culturally and linguistically diverse student?
4. How can students, parents, faculty, and staff who come from different countries maximize their fullest potential in Regina's "good" school?
5. Even though Regina is known as a "good" principal, should she not be retrained to be aware of current demographic changes taking place in schools and communities?

Consider Case 2, the case of Victor, a superintendent.

Case 2

A county school district had the reputation of maintaining quality and excellence in its "good" schools. Victor, its superintendent (frequently regarded as a "good" superintendent), did not believe in desegregation or the inclusion of minority and exceptional learners in school programs. In fact, his district did not respond to federal laws meant to address segregation. To achieve this aim of "quality without equity," Victor hired very well-paid, high-powered attorneys who were bent on maintaining this phony meritocratic standard.

Again, at first glance, Victor sounds like a man who believes in quality. However, a deeper look at the picture reveals a man who refuses to shift his paradigm and power with regard to racial and cultural valuing. The following pertinent questions should stimulate our thinking on our definition of good schools:

1. Does maintaining the status quo lead to "goodness" all the time?
2. How can minority students be treated with respect in this district?
3. How can learners with exceptionalities maximize their fullest potential in this district?
4. Why should the money wasted on the attorneys not be invested in *good* programming for *all* students?
5. Even though Victor is known as a "good" superintendent, should he not be retrained to be aware of current demographic changes taking place in schools and communities?

As we redefine good schools, we must make sure that the perspectives of principals and administrators are not ignored.

Again, it takes a good principal or good superintendent to develop a good school. We cannot downplay the impact of principals and school district administrators. As the late Dr. Martin Luther King, Jr. pointed out,

> Human progress is neither automatic nor inevitable. Even a superficial look at history reveals that no social advance rolls in on the wheels of inevitability. Every step toward the good of justice requires sacrifice, suffering, and struggle, the tireless exertions and passionate concern of dedicated individuals. Without persistent effort, time itself becomes an ally of the insurgent and primitive forces of irrational emotionalism and social destruction. This is no time for apathy or complacency. This is a time for vigorous and positive action. (C. King, 1983, p. 59)

Quality, Equity, and "Good" Schools

We need good schools, and we also need good teachers to make our students good learners, but our paradigms must shift if we are truly going to reach all students. In the words of Palmer (1998),

> Teaching, like any truly human activity, emerges from one's inwardness, for better or worse. As I teach, I project the condition of my soul into my students, my subject, and our way of being together. The entanglements of experience in the classroom are often no more or less than the convolutions of my inner life. Viewed from this angle, teaching holds a mirror to the soul. If I am willing to look at that mirror and not run from what I see, I have a chance to gain self-knowledge—and knowing myself is as crucial to good teaching as knowing my students and my subject. (p. 2)

"Good" schools should be where teachers and practitioners respond to cultural diversity. There is no doubt that cultural diversity enhances human relations. More than three decades ago, Henderson and Bibens (1970) noted,

> Human interactions in the classroom are generally of two types: teacher-student and student-student. The mood of the classroom is reflected in the words and behaviors of both the teachers and the students. Few educators would quarrel with the assumption that in order to minimize human relations problems in the classroom, skills related to identifying problems and finding their solutions should be taught to each student. All students should be able to distinguish between fact and opinion. Equally important, all students must be free to express their views. It is not enough to expose students to the opinions of "experts," they must be allowed to verbalize their opinions, no matter how "way out" they may seem. Much new understanding comes from hearing what others are saying. (p. 78)

"Good" schools should never be segregated environments where Blacks teach only Black students and Whites teach only White students. Such schools fail to prepare students for societal realities. Today, the sociocultural demography is changing, yet many students who come from different cultural, linguistic, and socioeconomic backgrounds become silenced, invisible voices that are misidentified, misassessed, miscategorized, misplaced, and misinstructed (Banks, 1999; Ford, Obiakor, & Patton, 1995; Grossman, 1998; Obiakor, 1994, 1999a, 1999b, 1999c; Obiakor et al., 1999; Obiakor & Utley, 1997). In urban, suburban, and rural schools, African American, Hispanic American, Asian American, and Native American students are now in schools with their Anglo American peers. These students can no longer be silenced, invisible voices. Also, the access to technology has made the world smaller. Although global competition has its own problems, global education is no longer a far-fetched idea. Interestingly, despite all the demographic changes taking place in schools today, the majority of teachers remain Anglo Americans. As a consequence, the burden falls on these teachers to be prepared to work with these different students. It seems clear that there is a "cultural disconnect" between these teachers and their students. Additionally, it seems clear that they must be culturally responsive in order to reach their students (Obiakor, 2000a, 2000b; Obiakor & Utley; Obiakor & Williams, 2000; Trent, Obiakor, Ford, & Artiles, 2000; Utley, Delquadri, Obiakor, & Mims, 2000). For instance, Utley et al. (2000) emphasized that responses to cultural diversity should be one indication of how good schools are. Banks (1999) explained that not including culture in our interpretation of good schools projects a utopian picture that is divorced from cultural, linguistic, and socioeconomic realities of our nation. He argued,

Multicultural education is needed to help all of the nation's future citizens to acquire the knowledge, attitudes, and skills needed to survive in the twenty-first century. Nothing less than the nation's survival is at stake. The rapid growth in the nation's population of people of color, the escalating importance of non-White nations such as China and Japan, and the widening gap between the rich and the poor make it essential for our future citizens to have multicultural literacy and cross-cultural skills. In the twenty-first century, a nation whose citizens cannot negotiate on the world's multicultural global stage will be tremendously disadvantaged, and its very survival may be imperiled. (p. 34)

Quality and equity must be integral parts of good schools. In other words, the education gained from good schools must have the power to enhance attitudes and intellectual sophistication (Dewey, 1958; Kohl, 1988). For instance, Dewey (1958) contended,

Education must have the tendency, if it is education, to form attitudes. The tendency to form attitudes which will express themselves in intelligent social action is something very different from indoctrination. . . . There is an intermediary between aimless education and the education of inculcation and indoctrination. The alternative is the kind of education that connects the materials and methods by which knowledge is acquired with a sense of how things are done: not by impregnating the individual with some final philosophy . . . but by enabling him [her] to so understand existing conditions that an attitude of intelligent action will follow from social understanding. (p. 56)

A logical extension is that social understandings are related to individual and societal valuing. Rather than devalue human beings, "good" schools must value the contributions of individuals to classroom and school cultures. Good schools therefore must be where individual beliefs, symbols, cultures, and languages are learned and incorporated into classroom daily functions. In other words, good schools and classrooms are not homogeneous environments that manifest exclusive practices divorced from individual and social freedoms. Good schools allow students to tell their stories. As Featherstone (1988) warned some years ago, "Unless we begin to hear each other's stories, we'll keep walking around like strangers in an airport. And we will certainly not provide the young with the guidance they need to end up doing something worthwhile that suits them" (p. ix). He added that "the interaction of children's minds and feelings with the curriculum is the true locus of good teaching and good learning; any approach that stresses the child at the expense of content, or the curriculum at the expense of the child, is simply unsound" (p. xii). In a nutshell, quality and equity must go hand-in-glove for schooling to be "good."

Altruism, Realities, and "Good" Schools

In "good" schools, teachers are professionals who take their jobs seriously. By tradition, teachers face different realities, and they have roles and subroles that they must play to maximize the potential of their students. Redl and Wattenberg

(1951) identified these roles and subroles of a teacher as including (a) representative of society (inculcates moral precepts),
(b) judge (evaluates), (c) helper (provides guidance for students), (d) referee (manages crises), (e) role model (possesses
traits that students imitate), (f) group leader (establishes classroom climate), (g) parent surrogate (acts as a parent), (h) friend
and confidante (establishes warm relationship with children
and shares confidences), and (i) object of affection (meets
psychological needs of students). Although good teachers
must be rewarded with merit pay and promotions, no amount
of money can compensate teachers for what they do. Put another way, good teachers are like good priests and pastors
who view their jobs spiritually and altruistically. Kohl (1988)
agreed that "the impulse to teach is fundamentally altruistic
and represents a desire to share what you value and to empower
others" (p. 7). He added,

> Wanting to teach is like wanting to have children or to
> write or paint or dance or invent or think through a
> mathematical problem that only a few have been able to
> solve. It has an element of mystery, involving as it does
> the yearly encounter with new people, the fear that you
> will be inadequate to meet their needs, as well as the
> rewards of seeing them become stronger because of your
> work. And as is true of the other creative challenges, the
> desire to teach and the ability to teach well are not the
> same thing. With the rarest of exceptions, one has to learn
> how to become a good teacher just as one has to learn how
> to become a scientist or an artist. (p. 16)

In many of our traditional "good" schools, some teachers
seem to have forgotten that teaching is a profession. As a
profession, it (a) performs an essential social service, (b) is
founded upon a systematic body of knowledge, (c) requires
a lengthy period of academic and practical training, (d) has a
high degree of autonomy, (e) has a code of ethics, and (f) gen-
erates inservice growth (Hoyle, 1975). Surprisingly, some
teachers in "good" schools do not (a) know who they are,

(b) learn the facts when they are in doubt, (c) change their thinking, (d) build self-concepts, (e) use resource persons, (f) teach with divergent techniques, (g) make the right choices, and (h) continue to learn (Obiakor, 1994). Rather, some of these teachers have politicized their professional activities. Some have stopped learning and, as a result, have refused to shift their paradigms. Following are questions that are critical to understanding what good schools entail:

1. Should "good" schools not be where good teaching involves positivism, flexibility, adaptability, sensitivity, and open-mindedness?

2. Should "good" schools not be where cultural, racial, linguistic, and socioeconomic heterogeneity reflect social realities?

3. Should "good" schools not be where student stressors and individual differences are responded to?

4. Should "good" schools not be where issues of student learning styles and multiple intelligences are addressed?

5. Should "good" schools not be where culturally diverse student, faculty, and staff populations are dedicated to excellence?

6. Should "good" schools not be where *all* students are encouraged to maximize their fullest potential?

7. Should "good" schools not be where parents and community members are empowered?

8. Should "good" schools not be where parents and teachers work collaboratively, consultatively, and cooperatively, despite their cultural, racial, linguistic, and socioeconomic differences?

9. Should "good" schools not be where students are educated for life and not suspended or expelled indiscriminately?

10. Should "good" schools not be where students are prepared to be responsible and productive citizens through self-knowledge, self-esteem, and self-empowerment?

11. Should "good" schools not be where students are prepared to be nationally and globally aware?

12. Should "good" schools not be where students' freedoms are maximized?

13. Should "good" schools not be where teachers foster human relations?

14. Should "good" schools not be where quality is incorporated with a "heart"?

15. Should "good" schools not be where student identification, assessment, placement, and instruction are nonrestrictive and nondiscriminatory?

16. Should "good" schools not be where communications flourish and different voices are heard?

Beyond Traditional "Good" Schools

On the whole, the undergirding spirit in "good" schools must be to prepare students for life's perfections and imperfections. Consider situations in Cases 3-5, three traditional "good" schools (Schools A, B, and C).

Case 3

School A was an elementary laboratory school that was attached to a university. As a laboratory school, preservice teachers were prepared in their field and practical experiences in this school. Interestingly, this school has failed twice in its quest to be a Charter School because of its lack of diversity in student, faculty, and staff populations. School A had mostly Anglo American students, faculty, and staff, and there was visible homogeneity in cultural, racial, linguistic, and socioeconomic backgrounds. In this school, cultural diversity or multicultural education was not infused in the general curricula. In fact, classes were held on the Martin Luther King, Jr. holiday. Also in this school, nobody had a visible physical disability, but some students took Ritalin because of attention deficit disorders. Fewer than 10 students were identified as having learning disabilities, especially in reading (i.e., dyslexia). School A's buildings were well-maintained, and classroom materials were readily available. In this school, there was zero tolerance for discipline problems, and students were easily punished and suspended without due process hearings or parental consent. There was a semi-alternative program for students with serious emotional disturbance located in the school's basement; however, School A tried to dissociate itself from this alternative program. Generally, teachers, administrators, and parents were happy that they produced students who made good grades and high scores on standardized norm-referenced tests.

Case 4

School B was a suburban elementary school that was culturally, racially, and socioeconomically homogeneous. However, some minority students were bussed from the city schools to respond to the issue of desegregation. School B had a majority of Anglo American teachers, staff, service providers, parents, and students. It also had one African American man who was the physical education teacher and an African American woman who was a permanent substitute teacher. Fewer than 10 minority students who came from middle- to upper-class homes attended this school from their suburban homes. Some students had learning disabilities, and a few of them were given Ritalin to deal with attention deficit disorders. In this school, there were a couple of students with visible mental or physical disabilities. There was also zero tolerance for discipline problems; however, the principal believed in parental involvement in students' daily activities. In this school, the Martin Luther King, Jr. holiday and Black History Month were observed. Cultural diversity was sometimes infused, but the lack of training of faculty and staff in this area seemed to create teacher-parent consultation and collaboration problems. School B prided itself on maintaining high student scores on standardized tests, and parents and community members were proud of the school's reputation.

Case 5

School C (frequently regarded as a "good" school) was a rural elementary school known for its belief in quality and excellence. It was culturally, racially, and socioeconomically homogeneous. However, it had a couple of students whose parents were migrant workers or worked in the beef factories. A handful of these students spoke little English (i.e., they were linguistically different). Because of this linguistic difference, they were put in special education programs. School C had many interesting policies. Examples include the following: (a) when students did not finish their work, they forfeited their recess periods; (b) when students finished all their work, they had "fun time," and those who were unable to finish were denied such fun time; (c) when students were tardy or absent, they were suspended, and if such tardiness continued, they were automatically expelled; (d) parental due process was not a top priority because parents were not allowed to infringe on school regulations; and (e) students were consistently tested to see if they had special education problems that would lead to early intervention and placement. In School C, cultural diversity was not an issue because the school never tried to address it—the focus was on student assimilation. Students from migrant families had no choice but to attend School C—it was the only one around. The other students (i.e., majority Anglo Americans) performed very well on standardized norm-referenced tests. School C focused solely on the 3 Rs (reading, writing, and arithmetic), and self-concept development activities were viewed as activities that "watered down" the curriculum. School C was popular in this school district.

It appears that Schools A, B, and C are typical "good" schools across the nation. Generally, we interpret their "goodness" on the basis of their students' performance on external exams. When we evaluate such schools, we manifest a pervasive puritanical mentality. We expect our schools to be perfect, our parents to be perfect, and our students to be perfect, notwithstanding life's imperfections. Yet we frequently forget that students, parents, and teachers are human elements of our imperfect society, and as a result, our puritanical expectations seem very unrealistic. A few years ago, O'Brien (1991) confirmed that "parents trying to raise respectful children today, unfortunately, have to do it in a disrespectful world. Brutal and hostile acts are shown in nightly television; profane, vulgar and irreverent language is used routinely in the media; greed and selfishness are revealed in important and prominent people; role models are too outrageous or too perfect to be taken seriously" (p. 183).

The critical question is this: How realistic are our "good" schools in addressing cultural, linguistic, and social demographics evident in the new millennium? School reform programs must emphasize quality and excellence; however, they also need to emphasize equity at all levels to present the kinds of realities that face students outside the school. Today's students deserve truly "good" schools because in such schools we have truly good teachers who (a) build their knowledge base, (b) examine the classroom culture, (c) plan and deliver classroom instruction, (d) negotiate the roles of teaching, (e) build self-concepts through self-efficacy, (f) restructure learning and work environments, (g) enhance learning with technologies and resources, (h) work beyond the classroom, and (i) shift paradigms in what they do (Obiakor, Karr, Utley, & Algozzine, 1998). In addition, our nation needs truly good teachers who are willing to meet their pedagogical challenges in today's classrooms by doing the following:

1. Saying what they mean and meaning what they say
2. Using time effectively and efficiently
3. Using information to indicate and create interest
4. Adopting and modifying instruction to respond to individual differences
5. Responding to cultural, linguistic, and socioeconomic differences
6. Teaching students to think
7. Making school fun
8. Making every student a winner
9. Evaluating student performance appropriately
10. Helping every child maximize his or her potential
11. Communicating properly with students, parents, and colleagues
12. Motivating their students toward self-responsibility
13. Rewarding their students
14. Mastering the art of questioning
15. Managing their classrooms

Strategic Lessons Learned

This chapter has foreshadowed ideas that are presented in the other chapters of the book; to a large measure, this chapter has dealt with specific classroom issues rarely addressed in an in-depth fashion. It is important that we begin to redefine what good schools and good classrooms mean if we are to survive as a society and nation. My premise is that many of our "good" schools cannot survive external scrutiny when evaluated from multidimensional perspectives. We need schools to practically manifest human realities—our definitions of good schools have been perceptually based and suffer from the problems that they are supposed to solve. Our good schools must respond to excellence and quality, but they must also respond to culture and socioeconomics. In the end, our good schools must be ones where teachers, principals, and administrators are prepared to move beyond tradition to expose all students to life's realities. Such a courageous move must be courageously supported by those who prepare teachers to be "good" through preservice and inservice trainings. We must have the courage to change from retrogressive traditionalism to progressive traditionalism. Just as we must honor our culture, we must also honor the world in which our culture exists. Teachers must honor our changing world to reach our unique students. As Palmer (1998) concluded,

> Teachers who use nontraditional methods feel thwarted by the traditionalism of their students, their students' parents, and some of their colleagues: "Stop doing the 'touchy-feely' stuff with students. Cover the field, make them memorize the facts, and show them how to compete. If you don't, you put them at disadvantage in the real world of work." . . . The irony is clear: the "real" world of work is the source of much pedagogical experimentation and change, precisely because conventional top-down teaching does not prepare students well for the realities of that world. But some students, some parents, and some academics are caught in a cultural lag. They need to hear the news. (pp. 178-179)

2

⊙~~⊙

Classroom
Identifications
and Referrals

It is common knowledge that the identification of students
affects how they are tested, placed, and instructed. Parents
rely on teachers' opinions in educational processes—they
take these opinions seriously. Ford et al. (1995), Obiakor et al.
(1999), and Rotatori and Obi (1999) agreed that teachers tend
to make idiosyncratic judgments on students' school and life
successes and failures, especially when they come from different cultural, linguistic, and socioeconomic backgrounds.
In their classic work more than three decades ago, Rosenthal
and Jacobson (1968) found that a positive relationship exists
between teacher expectation, differential treatment, and student self-fulfilling prophecy. Proctor (1984) confirmed that
"low expectations are generally associated with minority
group membership, low SES [socioeconomic status], male
gender, nonconformity personality, physical unattractiveness,
nonstandard speech patterns, and low achievement" (p. 122).

Many schools are trapped in the "good" school phenomenon. The presumption is that "good" schools have "good" teachers who make good judgments all the time. These teachers are assumed to know their "stuff." The important question is this: Are "good" teachers still good when they refuse to shift their paradigms, especially in the ways they identify or refer students because they look, behave, speak, and learn differently? Many teachers want to "get rid" of the uninterested students— they like to teach "good" students who make good scores on standardized tests. There is a danger in this kind of "good" school mentality. According to DeBruyn (1984),

> If we adopt a "get rid of" attitude, we violate a basic tenet of education: that each student is an individual, and that our instruction and curriculum must try to make allowances for individual differences. Regardless of our feelings, we cannot discount this tenet. That's why it is dangerous to adopt a practice that amounts to saying, "Get the uninterested, unmotivated, and ill-behaved out of the school to keep them from interfering with those who want to learn." In truth, this is an easy way out. And teaching all students is not easy. Yet, it remains our challenge. (p. 1)

In his book *The Mismeasure of Man*, Gould (1981) decried abuses associated with gross misidentification of the human potential based on "biological determinism." The idea of biological determinism is closely tied to the belief in racial superiority of one race over another (e.g., Whites over Blacks) (Herrnstein, 1971; Herrnstein & Murray, 1994; Jensen, 1973, 1985). When schools appear homogeneous, as many supposedly "good" schools consistently do, multiple intelligences are downplayed and almost "watered down," especially when students act, look, speak, and behave differently. Two questions come to mind. Should a "good" school not be an environment that allows for the fertilization and blooming of the multiple intelligences that students bring to school? Should a good teacher not allow these intelligences to bloom, in spite of cultural, linguistic, and socioeconomic differences? Gardner (1993) responded to these issues when he wrote,

> It is of the utmost importance that we recognize and nurture all of the varied human intelligences, and all of the combinations of intelligences. We are all so different largely because we all have different combinations of intelligences. If we recognize this, I think we will have at least a better chance of dealing appropriately with the many problems that we face in the world. If we can mobilize the spectrum of human abilities, not only will people feel better about themselves and more competent; it is even possible that they also feel more engaged and better able to join the rest of the world community in working for the broader good. Perhaps if we can mobilize the full range of human intelligences and ally them to an ethical sense, we can help to increase the likelihood of our survival on the planet and perhaps even contribute to our thriving. (p. 12)

In an era of desegregation, bussing students is a popular deal. The question of how "rich" schools welcome their "different" students still remains unanswered. Poverty is frequently associated with "poor" intelligence, "poor" home background, "poor" self-concept, and "poor" zest to survive in school and life. This myth of socioeconomic dissonance creates identification problems in supposedly "good" schools that "rich" students attend. Consider Case 6, based on Julius, a parent, recounting his experience with another parent (one of those "good" parents) whose child attended a "good" school.

Case 6

Julius was involved in a conversation about quality education with another parent and principal associated with a "good" suburban school. Julius was an African American parent, and both the other parent and the principal were Anglo Americans. Their conversation was intellectual, deep, and meaningful, and they felt good about their conclusions. Before leaving the room, the other parent expressed joy that the school was great but said that the taxes in the suburban village were too much. Julius and the principal agreed. In addition, Julius responded, "Everything is worth it. The taxes are needed to recruit and hire quality teachers and buy school materials and equipment." The other parent responded to Julius with anger and said, "Speak for yourself! You do not live here so you will not understand what I mean by too much taxes." Julius and the principal were shocked because they had presumed that through their conversations the other parent would have deduced that they all lived in this suburb.

Five questions are critical to consider regarding the "good" school phenomenon. If a parent is this ignorant, what do we expect from his child? How will such a parent encourage his children to relate to those "different" children who are bussed to this suburban school? How will this other parent work with other parents who are not visibly rich? Is it not obvious that this parent, even with his wealth, is "poor" spiritually and intellectually? Should a "good" school not help educate its parents, patrons, supporters, and sponsors? These questions are strongly tied to how "different" students are identified and referred.

In the example presented above, the other parent misidentified Julius. He thought that because Julius was an African American man he could not afford to live in the expensive suburban homes. He was trapped by the dangerous myth of socioeconomic dissonance. He was also trapped by his belief on race. In other words, race still mattered to him (see West, 1993). Are all Blacks "poor?" Or are all Whites "rich?" By the way, what does *poverty* mean? And what does *richness* mean? Our definitions of these constructs must go beyond our traditional perspectives. The fact remains that our educational programs have been trapped by deficit-oriented constructs that set limits on the maximization of the human capital.

Should "good" schools not be where teachers address these constructs and their meanings to suit human realities? Consider the following pertinent cases.

Case 7

Mary is an experienced kindergarten teacher in a "good" elementary school. In her kindergarten class is Paul, the only African American student in the class. Paul's father has a doctorate degree, and his mother has a master's degree. They both work at a major university. Mary was teaching alphabets A-Z and word associations to her kindergarten class (e.g., "a for apple," "b for ball," "c for cat," "d for dog," etc.). In the first parent-teacher conference, Mary told the parent that although Paul is a good student he is quiet in class. According to Mary, "Such quietness is a red flag for academic and behavior problems. As a result, I am recommending that you [the parent] take advantage of the Chapter One Program for students from poor and disadvantaged backgrounds like Paul. The Chapter One Program will help him work on his reading deficit early. I have many years of experience; I know a problem when I see one. My gut feeling has never failed me." Paul's parent was shocked. The next day he brought a second-grade reading book and asked Paul to read in Mary's presence. She was surprised that Paul could read and that she had misidentified him. Paul's parent responded, "I'm the one who asked him to be quiet in school. How can you identify a reading problem when you are still teaching alphabets and word associations? Don't you think you need more education on the issue of culture?" Mary never apologized for misidentifying Paul. Rather, she spent the school year trying to prove that she was correct by finding little faults. Because of this kind of witch-hunt, Mary's classroom environment was a restrictive one for Paul, and his parents had to remove him from this school to avoid more damage to his self-concept. Throughout the year, opportunities to collaborate and consult were not maximized because Mary and Paul's parents never got along.

Traditional Problems and Solutions

In Case 7, there are apparent problems that include the following:

1. Mary might have been an experienced teacher; however, she lacked the cultural competence to deal with Paul, the only African American student in the class.
2. Mary was unable to respond to Paul's individual differences in culture, language, and style.
3. Mary identified Paul wrongly. She was engaging in iatrogenic teaching (i.e., creating a classroom problem that did not exist before).
4. Mary's collaboration with Paul's parents was in jeopardy.
5. Mary's perceptual assumptions led her to make prejudicial statements and draw illusory conclusions.
6. Because of Mary's expectations of Paul, her classroom environment became noticeably restrictive for him. He could not maximize his fullest potential in the class.
7. Mary never had the courage to actually teach Paul.

Traditionally, some teachers find it difficult to resolve classroom conflicts caused by their misinterpretations. They tend to be defensive and fail to apologize because they want to prove that they are right. As indicated, Mary felt that her experiences were enough for her to identify Paul's inability to read. This behavior is very typical in schools. Rather than acknowledge her misidentification, she spent the whole year trying to prove her point. Sadly, many so-called good teachers "play God"—they stop learning because they do not believe there are new ideas out there. The "one-size-fits-all" solution is traditionally pervasive in supposedly "good" schools.

Culturally Responsive Solutions

Many "good" teachers in many "good" schools tend to be unidimensionally knowledgeable. For example, in Case 7, Mary had the knowledge and experience. However, as it stands, experience is not always the best teacher. Based on Case 7, I believe a truly good teacher should do the following:

1. Apologize and not play God when he or she is wrong
2. Respond to individual differences, not just interindividual differences (differences between people), but also intraindividual differences (differences within people)
3. Learn more about the student's culture and learning style
4. Learn about the student's parents
5. Collaborate, consult, and cooperate with parents, because "it takes a responsible village to raise a responsible child"
6. Make his or her instructional environment least restrictive to allow students to maximize their fullest potential
7. Never misidentify his or her student, instead focusing on teaching first and judging later
8. Be flexible, sensitive, and caring
9. Continue to learn how to modify his or her instructions
10. Look for ways to uplift students' spirits rather than looking for ways to denigrate them

Key Points

Based on the aforementioned details, here are some important key points:

1. Teaching is a field that involves the "soul" and spirituality.
2. Teaching involves the courage to do what is right.
3. Teaching involves self-knowledge and self-empowerment.
4. Teaching involves cultural competence and cultural valuing.

5. Teaching involves the ability to manipulate the learning environment.

Case 8

Emilia was a 14-year-old immigrant from Mexico. She was bussed to a "good" suburban school. She had been in the United States for only three months. She was experiencing some difficulties with the English language while trying to adjust to the American culture. She was new and had not made friends in the school. She did not want to sound different, and therefore she did not participate in class. She was shy and isolated herself from her peers. She rarely participated in class and seemed to have trouble getting started with her classwork. Martha, her teacher, acknowledged that Emilia was very respectful and polite and had tried several times to engage her in conversation but that Emilia said very little each time. It was six weeks into the school year, and Martha was still not able to get much information from her. Martha was very concerned that Emilia was failing to adjust well in school activities, and thus she recommended that Emilia be tested for attention deficit disorder or emotional disturbance.

Traditional Problems and Solutions

In Case 8, there are apparent problems that include the following:

1. Although bussing helps schools combat segregation, students like Emilia frequently encounter psychosocial problems from peers and teachers.
2. Emilia's adjustment problems were misconstrued as emotional disturbance.
3. The burden of making friends was placed on Emilia by the teacher, Martha.

4. Emilia's inability to participate or concentrate in class was misjudged as attention deficit disorder.

5. Martha failed to do all she could for Emilia before categorizing her.

6. Martha did not consult and collaborate with Emilia's parents for identification.

7. Martha did not value the cultural and linguistic differences that Emilia brought to class.

Traditionally, some teachers find it difficult to respond to cultural and linguistic differences. As indicated, Martha was not concerned that Emilia was an immigrant adjusting to the educational system in the United States. She never tried to consult and collaborate with the parents to see how the problem could be ameliorated. Clearly, her desire was to get rid of this supposedly antisocial student in her class without understanding that doing so could create more devastating problems for her "new" student.

Culturally Responsive Solutions

Many teachers in presumed "good" schools think they have nothing new to learn. In Case 8, Martha has the knowledge for how to improve her students' grades and scores on standardized norm-referenced tests. But her insensitivity to cultural and linguistic differences is obvious. Based on Case 8, I believe a truly good teacher should do the following:

1. Be sensitive to cultural and linguistic differences

2. Not quickly identify students as having problems that they do not have

3. Positively manipulate his or her instructional environment

4. Consult and collaborate with parents before making judgments

5. Not try to "get rid of" his or her students

6. Understand the concepts of intraindividual differences (differences within individuals) and interindividual differences (differences between individuals)
7. Honor his or her profession
8. Teach with some "soul"
9. Practicalize "quality with a heart"
10. Value the values of his or her students by not looking at them from a deficit perspective

Key Points

Based on the aforementioned details, here are some important key points:

1. Teaching involves learning and growth.
2. Teaching and learning cannot be divorced from each other.
3. Teaching involves the manipulation of the learning environment.
4. Teaching involves helping every student maximize his or her potential.
5. Teaching involves courage, ethics, and integrity.

Case 9

Jason was a 10-year-old Asian American boy who attended a "good" school. His attendance had been very regular, and he made good grades in his classes. He was very sociable and got along well with his peers. His demeanor began to change, and he became frequently angry and resentful. He lost his temper easily and often argued with his teacher, Vickie. He got frustrated with the teacher when she tried to talk to him, and sometimes he was rebellious. Vickie came to the counselor and reported, "I am worried about Jason. I am referring him for testing. I believe he is emotionally disturbed." The counselor tried to contact Jason's parents and discovered that they were going through a divorce. They were engaged in an ugly court battle over the children and their properties. There was no peace at home, and Jason was considering running away.

Traditional Problems and Solutions

In Case 9, there are apparent problems, including the following:

1. Jason suffered from what many Asian Americans go through (i.e., the "model minority syndrome").
2. Jason's crisis was misconstrued as emotional disturbance.
3. Vickie's expectations of Jason were not realistic. Is it any wonder that Jason was misidentified?
4. Vickie did not maintain consistent collaborative activities with Jason's parents.
5. Vickie failed to contact Jason's parents before talking with the counselor. There is a problem of betraying confidential information.
6. Jason's stressors needed to be addressed to affect emotional intelligence.
7. The focus on classroom academic performance took precedence over Jason's crisis.

As we can see, Jason was misidentified because his home problems were affecting his school performance. The traditional solution is to downplay Jason's problems and get rid of him in the classroom because he has ceased to be a model minority student. Even "good" teachers are quick to misidentify "good" students. Traditionally, the focus is on academics alone and not on the whole child—this practice is seriously unidimensional.

Culturally Responsive Solutions

Case 9 exposes a student who was crying for help. This young student was going through some disruption and crisis in his life, yet no one was listening! Based on Case 9, I believe a truly "good" teacher should do the following:

1. Teach the whole child
2. Not overestimate or underestimate his or her student's capability
3. Be confidential in addressing the student's problem
4. Understand how students from different cultural groups (e.g., Asian Americans) handle crises
5. Be an active listener
6. Focus on emotional intelligence just as he or she focuses on intelligence quotient scores
7. Be sensitive to the needs of the student
8. Collaborate and consult with students' parents
9. Be flexible as he or she modifies the learning environment
10. Continue to learn through inservice training

Key Points

Based on the aforementioned details, here are some important key points:

1. Teaching involves knowing how different cultural groups respond to crises.
2. Teaching involves crisis management.
3. Teaching involves flexibility and sensitivity.
4. Teaching involves the "heart and soul."
5. Teaching involves confidentiality of information.

Case 10

Delvin was a 12-year-old Native American boy who attended a "good" school. He was of average intelligence and performed at his grade level. He was very mechanical and enjoyed taking things apart and putting the pieces back together. He wanted to be an automobile mechanic when he finished high school. His family was financially poor. He wore worn and dirty clothes. He appeared sick and tired most of the time and often slept in class. He did not get along well with his peers because they ridiculed him and called him derogatory names. John, his teacher, was worried that Delvin snapped easily and lost control. For this reason, he referred Delvin to be tested for emotional disturbance.

Traditional Problems and Solutions

In Case 10, there are apparent problems that include the following:

1. Delvin was misidentified because of his socioeconomic background.
2. Poverty, in this instance, was misconstrued as "poor" behavior.
3. John downplayed the derogatory comments of Delvin's peers.
4. There was no mutual respect in John's class.
5. John was unable to foster cooperative learning between Delvin and his peers.
6. Delvin was an "invisible man" (Ellison, 1972) in his class, and the teacher was unaware of how to give him a positive voice in class.
7. John had given up on Delvin, and the next step was to refer him for testing for emotional disturbance.

Traditionally, students like Delvin have a difficult time surviving in "good" schools. He had two strikes against him—both his cultural and his socioeconomic backgrounds are different. To his teacher, he did not belong in this "good" school, and as a result, he needed to be placed in a class for students with emotional disturbance. It is amazing that Delvin's teacher was dumbfounded when it came to dealing with those who ridiculed Delvin. Such silence is traditionally intentional—it is one way to make the student invisible.

Culturally Responsive Solutions

Case 10 presents a student of average intelligence who performed at his grade level. As indicated, he was a Native American student whose family was financially not very well-to-do. But his negative experiences could have been combated. Based on Case 10, I believe a truly good teacher should do the following:

1. Know that "poverty" is not synonymous with "poor" intelligence or "poor" ability to succeed in life
2. Not allow his or her student to be ridiculed
3. Make his or her instructional environment least restrictive
4. Have the courage to manage his or her class effectively
5. Learn the facts when he or she is in doubt
6. Accurately enhance the self-concepts of his or her students
7. Not engage in the wrong referral of students
8. Not defer his or her responsibilities
9. Infuse cultural understanding in his or her class
10. Empower his or her students, in spite of their socioeconomic backgrounds

Key Points

Based on the aforementioned details, here are some important key points:

1. Teaching involves self-knowledge of strengths and weaknesses.
2. Teaching can never be divorced from the enhancement of self-concepts.
3. Teaching involves empathy and kindness.
4. Teaching involves cultural sensitivity.
5. Teaching involves the manipulation of the learning environment.

Strategic Lessons Learned

This chapter has presented the dangers of inappropriate identification and referral of students, especially those who come from different cultural, linguistic, and socioeconomic backgrounds. My premise is that good schools are environments where "good" teachers respond to the following identification and referral principles:

1. All identifications and referrals must be appropriate.
2. Inappropriate identifications lead to labels and categories.
3. Identifications and referrals influence assessments of students.
4. Personal idiosyncrasies affect how students are identified.
5. Perceptions affect student identifications and referrals, which in turn create illusory generalizations.
6. Race matters in identifications and referrals.
7. Prejudice affects poor identification and referral procedures.
8. The more we care for people, the more we care about how we identify their strengths and weaknesses.
9. When identifications are done correctly, we see the "good" and "bad" in students.
10. Good identification and good teaching go hand in hand.
11. Cultural incompetence can lead to misidentification and misreferral.

12. Cultural valuing leads to self-valuing, which in turn leads to the valuing of others.

13. In good classrooms, students are identified on the basis of who they are without prejudicial expectations.

14. Expectations, when they are *realistic*, lead to proper qualifications and quantifications of human behavior.

15. It takes a collaborative and consultative team to properly identify students' strengths and weaknesses.

3

Classroom
Assessments
and Accountabilities

Assessment has become synonymous with accountability in today's schools. Schools are regarded as "good" when their students score high on standardized norm-referenced tests. Interestingly, the more the public demands accountability, the more narrowly we think about assessment. This phony meritocratic ideal transcends all educational policies and activities in today's schools. To a large measure, the underlying engine behind the "good" school phenomenon is assessment.

It is common knowledge that the assessment process is traditionally biased against individuals whose gender, race, ethnic background, culture, religion, or disability includes or excludes them from receiving a service or participating in an opportunity because of their nondominant status in mainstream Anglo society (Midgette, 1995; Obiakor & Schwenn, 1996). For instance, Obiakor and Schwenn (1996) confirmed that for culturally and linguistically diverse students with different behavioral patterns, assessment abuses have resulted in inappropriate interpretations, classifications, labels, and dysfunctional educational programming. Over the years, abuses in assessment issues have been well documented. About two decades ago, Salvia and Ysseldyke (1981) wrote,

> When one considers the abuses that have occurred in psychological assessment, it is easy to lose sight of the fact that the intentions of the testing establishment (testers and decision makers who use test data) are benevolent. The abuses that have occurred are a result of ignorance and overzealousness. The most crucial uses and frequently the most serious abuses of tests are those that involve decisions about individual children: screening, placement, program planning, and the evaluation of individual pupil progress. Inappropriate testing for these purposes can result in wasted time, and, more importantly, inappropriate classification and labeling and inappropriate educational programs. (pp. 532-533)

Assessment takes into account the overall evaluation of a student and therefore differs in concept from testing. Because tests are only samples of behavior, assessment includes more than testing (Witt, Elliot, Kraub, & Gresham, 1994). In fact, school-based assessment involves collecting and synthesizing information about a problem. According to Witt et al. (1994), assessment is

> an ongoing process which involves a wide array of materials, techniques, and tests across a variety of time periods and situations. Teachers, parents, counselors, psychologists, speech clinicians, and even children can be involved actively in the process of assessing their strengths and weaknesses at school or home. Thus assessment, particularly for purposes of special or remedial education, is multifaceted and should be a team process

whereby professionals and laypersons work cooperatively toward the solution of a problem. (p. 5)

Based on this statement by Witt et al., assessment should be
multidimensional. However, traditional assessment in traditional "good" schools has been limited to the use of normal-
ized standardized tests for a person who looks, acts, and
speaks differently. Selections of tests to be used for diagnosis
have ignored societal changes, cultural diversity, and changes
in children's needs. Karr and Wright (1995) argued,

Although the utilization of traditional assessment is
essential for individuals with problem behaviors, a
broader base approach appears to be of more use in today's changing society. Educators' awareness of the
need to utilize more contemporary assessment procedures calls for a more holistic approach to address the
needs of our ever changing multicultural society. (p. 64)

Each year in America's schools, more than 250 million standardized tests are administered to compare students' results
to the norms (Anastasi, 1976). Diagnostic, formative, and
summative evaluations have been deemed necessary to determine the effectiveness of a student's program. Diagnostic
tests are given before the individual student's program is
initiated, formative tests are given during the intervention,
and summative tests are given after the intervention has been
completed. It is clear that much time and effort are devoted to
the development of assessment tools (Elksnin, Larsen, &
Wallace, 1992). However, their use continues to raise numer-
ous questions. For instance, how reliable and valid are these
tools to students who are culturally and linguistically diverse?
How have test results been used to interpret accurately or
inaccurately these students' abilities? How have these interpretations been beneficial in placing, categorizing, and in-
structing culturally and linguistically diverse students? Tests
are reliable when the results of assessment are consistent, yet
many tests fail to produce consistent results. Even when tests
produce consistent results, they may still fail to define the

construct they purport to measure (Grilliot, 1995; Obiakor, 1992, 1999c; Obiakor, Harris-Obiakor, Obi, & Eskay, 2000). A critical question must then be asked: Can an instrument measure a construct that has not been defined? One cannot presume that everyone understands the construct measured by tests when the construct is not defined. More than a decade ago, Kauffman (1989) revealed that

nearly all behavioral standards and expectations—and therefore nearly all judgements regarding behavior deviance—are culture-bound; value judgements cannot be entirely culture-free. In our pluralistic society, which values multicultural elements, the central question for educators is whether they have made sufficient allowance in their judgement for behavior that is a function of a child's particular cultural heritage. (p. 212)

Because assessments are used to determine which are "good" schools, a more comprehensive, holistic model of assessment has been suggested. Park, Pullis, Reilly, and Townsend (1994) explained that "(1) concerted efforts aimed at developing and using culturally relevant assessment instruments and practices should occur, and (2) recruitment, preparation, and retention of a more diverse and multiculturally competent population of personnel to serve students with behavioral disorders should also occur . . . teachers, diagnosticians, administrators, and university personnel" (p. 24). Additionally, the holistic model (see Karr & Wright, 1995, pp. 66-67) must include the following:

1. *Information Sources* (e.g., teacher, administrators, parents/guardians, children, and other pertinent school personnel)
2. *Environment* (e.g., home, school, whole class, and structured activities behaviors)

3. *Data Sources* (e.g., structured interview, observation, behavior rating scale, psychological test, checklist, and specialized informal/formal test)
4. *Comprehensive Responses* (e.g., conferences, program design, duration of services, follow-up services, and reassessment of program and service semiannually)

School accountability is great as long as it does not only entail assessment that diminishes human value. Our traditional "good" schools tend to diminish the multidimensional nature of students' strengths and thus to diminish human value. A few years ago, Goodlad (1993) decried this behavior when he wrote,

> We appear incapable of getting beyond individuals as the units of assessment with the accompanying allocation of responsibility for success and failure. We must adopt as standard practice the kind of contextual appraisal that tells whether schools have in place the curriculum, materials, pedagogy, and other conditions necessary to the good education of individuals. The absence of these exposes glaring inequities that are the moral responsibility of a caring people in a just society to correct. (p. 20)

It does not make educational sense to use unreliable assessments to identify students with learning, social, or behavioral problems. Efforts to reduce the overrepresentation of certain groups of students, especially minorities, in special education settings must be taken seriously (Artiles & Trent, 1994; Obiakor & Algozzine, 1995). Inclusive classrooms must evolve, and such classrooms must be taught by knowledgeable educators who value the differing experiences and backgrounds of their students. Students cannot be misjudged because they look and act differently. According to Hilliard (1992),

1. We must assume that children's thinking can be changed significantly. We do not know their upper limits.

2. We are interested in processes of thinking and how they can be changed, rather than in the product for comparative purposes (ranking and classification).

3. We must require that any system that is employed be able to produce significant and meaningful change in students' cognitive and academic functioning.

4. We should, given the existence of a successful system, have a theoretical explanation of it. (p. 70)

Based on the aforementioned details, it is logical to conclude that assessments have become an integral part of today's educational activities. As a consequence, it is imperative that teachers who are truly good shift their paradigms about assessment. To practicalize this perspective, truly good teachers must make assessments that are as follows:

1. Instructionally related and curriculum based

2. Operational and functional

3. Authentic and realistic

4. Nondiscriminatory

5. Multidimensional

6. Nonjudgmental and meaningful

7. Responsive to intraindividual and interindividual differences and styles

8. Unemotional, area specific, and situation specific

9. Consultative and collaborative

10. Accurate, reliable, and valid

11. Responsive to observable variables

12. Ethically and morally responsive

13. Full of "soul"

14. Holistic

15. Germane to culture, race, environment, and language

These ideas were encapsulated in the 1997 Individuals With Disabilities Education Act (IDEA 1997, Pub. L. 105-17). According to IDEA amendments, local education agencies are required to conduct functional behavior assessments to determine the antecedent behaviors, behaviors, and consequences for students who exhibit atypical behaviors. As McConnell, Hilvitz, and Cox (1998) pointed out,

> Functional assessment can be used to determine possible cause(s) of a student's behavior so that interventions and modifications in the instructional environment can be developed and put into place, as specifically expressed in a student's Behavioral Intervention Plan. This is done in an attempt to reduce and/or extinguish the problem behavior while retaining instructional integrity in the student's educational program. The classroom teacher serves as the assessment facilitator and is responsible for initiating the process, completing the assessment, collecting data, and implementing the Behavior Intervention Plan. (p. 11)

A critical analysis of this statement by McConnell et al. (1998) is that the classroom teacher is an important element in the assessment process and that he or she works with a multi-disciplinary team (e.g., special education teacher, general education administrator, school psychologist, counselor, special education administrator, support personnel, and parents). To a large extent, the regular classroom teacher should encourage different perspectives because they affect best practices. The truly "good" teacher ought to see assessment as a functional, team-oriented process that gathers information on the relationship between the behavior and the environment. McConnell et al. noted that "direct observation is an important component of the functional assessment process" (p. 11). In other words, the classroom teacher has the important job of counting "the frequency of behavioral occurrences, the duration of the behavior, and/or the intensity of the behavior" (p. 11). As a result, the teacher's integrity and ethics are important in the assessment process—he or she is trusted to uphold the law and to document behaviors unprejudicially as prescribed by Public Law 105-17 (IDEA 1997). The question is, shouldn't good schools be where teachers do not betray this legal trust? Consider the following pertinent cases.

Case 11

Linus was a 12th-grade African American student who attended a "good" school. He was pretty good in mathematics but did not enjoy reading. He had taken the state assessment test several times without passing scores. Even though it was not uncommon to see this in schools, the teacher and parent put pressure on Linus, and the principal put pressure on Linus's teacher. Linus's mother understood that he could not graduate unless he passed this state test. His mother wanted to know if there was anything the counselor could do to help him graduate at the end of the year because he needed to move on with his life. She informed the counselor that she had been advised by her friend that if Linus were placed in a special education program he would not be required to pass the state test before getting his high school diploma. She therefore wanted to know if the counselor could simply change Linus's placement to special education. This would ease all the assessment anxieties for Linus, his parent, his teacher, and his principal.

Traditional Problems and Solutions

In Case 11, there are apparent problems, including the following:

1. Linus had the typical problem of not enjoying reading, yet he was pretty good in mathematics.
2. Linus felt the pressure of state-approved standardized testing.

3. Linus's teacher and mother felt pressured by the administrator.

4. The classroom performance of Linus in mathematics was downplayed.

5. Linus's test-taking skills were defining whether he should graduate or not.

6. Linus's mother was suggesting that he be placed in a special education program in order to ease the assessment tension.

7. Everything that Linus had learned in school was at risk of not being considered in framing his school and future success.

Traditionally, schools have relied on standardized norm-referenced tests as good predictor variables of how well students will succeed in life. This excessive reliance on standardized test scores is a dangerous phenomenon. There is the underlying thinking that everyone has to go to college. If college graduates are always the most successful in life, then the "Unabomber" (the man who killed many people with packaged bombs) would have amounted to something greater, Einstein would not have been a well-known and successful mathematician, and Bill Gates would not have become one of the richest men in the world. It is unfortunate that traditional "good" schools have relied solely on students' performance on norm-referenced tests, even when we know they lack reliability (a test's ability to produce consistent results) and validity (a test's ability to measure what it purports to measure). Sadly, we have become slaves to those tests in these days of school accountability.

Culturally Responsive Solutions

As indicated, many good teachers in good schools rely solely on standardized tests to predict how successful students will be in future education and life opportunities. In Case 11, Linus's classroom performance was not considered in the same dimension that his performance on standardized tests was considered. Based on Case 11, I believe a truly "good" teacher should do the following:

1. Learn that standardized tests lack reliability and validity, especially for students who are culturally and linguistically diverse
2. Respond to individual differences in test-taking skills
3. Teach parents that standardized tests are not good predictor variables of how individuals will succeed in school, job, and life
4. Explain that even when tests produce consistent results, they do not always measure what they purport to measure
5. Summarize that good tests are not divorced from good classroom instructions
6. Practicalize the "Teach Test Reteach and Retest Model," which equitably incorporates both teaching and testing in learning activities
7. Work collaboratively and consultatively with parents in the assessment and accountability processes
8. Regard assessment as a functional teamwork process that recognizes the relationship between behavior and the environment
9. Reduce the "soullessness" of assessments, that is, not be a slave to assessments
10. Assess students with a "heart" and respond to cultural, linguistic, and socioeconomic variables that students bring to school

Key Points

Based on the aforementioned details, here are some important key points:

1. Teaching involves the knowledge of assessment.
2. Teaching and assessment are not divorced from each other.

3. In teaching, assessment should predict what the student has learned and how the student can be taught.

4. Teaching involves direct observations of human behaviors.

5. Teaching involves nonprejudicial and nondiscriminatory information-gathering systems.

Case 12

Garcia was a 10-year-old boy who had lived in the United States for 10 years. He attended a "good" school. Although his family spoke primarily Spanish in the home, Garcia spoke moderate English. Peers frequently ridiculed Garcia's English—they felt he was not "smart" because of his slight accent—and he had difficulty relating to them. Classmates consistently used negative words to describe him. Garcia's parents had tried working with the classroom teacher. However, this teacher had frequently ignored them and had taken the side of the peers. On one occasion, the teacher noted that "Garcia is a bad kid who does nothing right." Garcia was referred by this teacher for standardized testing for behavior disorders. The night before the assessment, Garcia's dog was hit by a car and killed. He therefore was in poor spirits to take the tests, yet he was assessed as scheduled. On the testing date, the school psychologist, who spoke no Spanish, was grouchy because of car problems on the way to school. The tests were administered in her small office, a place unfamiliar to Garcia. Test scores were compared to Anglo norms. In the interpretation of scores, Garcia's cultural, linguistic, and emotional aspects were not considered. In the end, Garcia was labeled "behavior disordered" and placed in the special education program. Variables such as cultural differences, academic background, ability to speak and understand English, negative peer behavior, the uncooperativeness of the general education teacher, emotional concerns of losing the pet, and the grouchiness of the examiner were not considered in the identification and assessment of behavior disorders for Garcia.

Traditional Problems and Solutions

In Case 12, there are apparent problems that include the following:

1. Peer harassment of Garcia was downplayed by his teacher. Her comment that he was a "bad kid" was also a form of teacher harassment.
2. Garcia's self-concept and psychological problems in the class did not seem to matter.
3. Assessment was used to label Garcia rather than to improve instruction.
4. Garcia's teacher seemed to believe that Garcia was the problem. As a result, she wanted to get rid of him.
5. Assessment was totally divorced from Garcia's learning style.
6. Garcia's teacher seemed to downplay the concept of intraindividual and interindividual differences.
7. The unprofessional behavior of Garcia's test giver was ignored.

Traditionally, it appears that teachers use standardized norm-referenced tests to get rid of students they do not like. Garcia's case is an excellent example of a teacher who did not care about the emotional intelligence of all her students. The students who harassed Garcia knew no better, but his teacher should have known better. Many culturally and linguistically diverse students find themselves in schools that downplay their strengths while highlighting their weaknesses. Cultural differences appear to have been misconstrued by Garcia's classmates and teacher. Of what use is an assessment if it fails to connect with classroom instruction? The teacher's inability to manipulate the learning environment is a big problem— the sad consequences are the suggestion that Garcia be tested and the label that ensued. Again, we see the dangers of the excessive reliance on tests that fail to produce consistent results or fail to measure what they purport to measure. The critical question is this: How has Garcia's teacher helped him maximize his fullest potential?

Culturally Responsive Solutions

Many "good" teachers in "good" schools use assessments as vindictive weapons to get rid of students they do not like. Sadly, they use them when they view students from deficit perspectives. In Case 12, Garcia was viewed as a distraction in classroom activities even though he had been consistently harassed by his teacher and peers. Evidently, teachers can see what they want to see in students. Based on Case 12, I believe a truly "good" teacher should do the following:

1. Not harass his or her students
2. Learn the power of words—words can heal, but they can also hurt
3. Not devalue his or her students
4. Be careful about using an assessment instrument that does not help him or her in classroom instruction
5. Use assessments for the right reasons (i.e., to find out how students are learning in the classroom)
6. Not label his or her students and should instead get to know them
7. Not use assessments to label or get rid of his or her students
8. Manipulate the learning environment to suit all of his or her students
9. Be careful about using an assessment to compare his or her students to other students
10. Not abuse tests or use tests to abuse his or her students

Key Points

Based on the aforementioned details, here are some important key points:

1. Teaching involves the manipulation of the learning environment.
2. Teaching entails respect for human differences.
3. Teaching, when done right, incorporates students' learning styles and cultural backgrounds.
4. Teaching should incorporate emotional intelligence.
5. Teaching, when done right, reduces the "soullessness" of assessment.

Case 13

Jenny was an Asian American student who attended a "good" suburban school. She excelled in her school work. On one occasion, Jenny and her classmates were given a reading assignment by their teacher. This reading assignment entailed producing a book report, but Jenny missed the due date for some reason. Her father disciplined her when this was brought to his attention. He sent a personal note that indicated "This will never never happen again!" He also made Jenny send a letter of apology to the teacher. In addition, Jenny finished her assignment and submitted it the next day. Jenny finished other subsequent assignments earlier than due dates. When the quarterly grade was sent home, the teacher graded Jenny's reading as "incomplete." Jenny's father was displeased by this result, and Jenny, on her part, was devastated and discouraged because there is a big difference between late work and incomplete work. This created some mistrust between Jenny's father and the teacher and Jenny and the teacher.

Traditional Problems and Solutions

In Case 13, there are apparent problems that include the following:

1. Even though Jenny missed the due date of her reading assignment, her teacher did not try to learn the reasons for her missing the due date.
2. Jenny's teacher failed to communicate with Jenny's parent.
3. The trusts of Jenny and her father were betrayed by the teacher. Jenny's apology and her father's note to the teacher were ignored.
4. Jenny's hard work throughout the quarter was downplayed.
5. The "incomplete" grade falsely suggested that Jenny did not complete her work. There is a difference between lateness and incompleteness.
6. The "incomplete" grade sounded punitive and failed to recognize the total performance of Jenny.
7. There was the underlying motive of teaching Jenny a lesson (i.e., the "three strikes you're out" mentality).

Traditionally, as in Case 13, assessment appears to be used for punitive purposes (i.e., you miss the due date, you're ruined). How does the evaluation of the student fit the student's capability? Therein lies the problem! The summative use of assessments frequently fails to indicate diagnostic and formative aspects of a student or program. This seems to create inconsistent and unnecessary complexities in the student's evaluation. As a test giver, the teacher failed to understand the circumstances surrounding the student's ability or inability. What kind of environment is set for the student? How can the student maximize her potential in this kind of classroom? Certainly such a classroom is a restrictive one where students and their parents feel less empowered. The student's apology and the parent's note to the teacher were both ignored. How can positive collaboration and consultation be maintained in such a classroom?

Culturally Responsive Solutions

Many "good" teachers fail to see the big picture with respect to assessment. They view assessment unidimensionally instead of multidimensionally. Assessments must be broad enough to involve interviews, work samples, observations, portfolios, and other classroom-based activities. Additionally, they must not be divorced from instructions that take place in learning environments. In Case 13, Jenny's "incomplete" grade demonstrated an evaluation that did not reflect her ability or potential. In an attempt to maintain *quality*, such a practice actually destroys *quality*. Based on Case 13, I believe a truly "good" teacher should do the following:

1. Focus on the needs of his or her student across all components of the ecological system in which he or she learns

2. Emphasize instruction as the primary purpose of assessment

3. Not use assessment as a punitive measure

4. Practice assessment as an ongoing process that is best conducted in the teaching-learning situation

5. Not extrapolate from limited samples of behavior

6. Learn that intelligence and performance are not static

7. Learn that the task of assessment is to pinpoint where students are, what they can do, and what they are doing, *not* what they cannot do

8. Not abuse tests or use tests to abuse (or discriminate against) students

9. View culture and language as embodiments of assessment

10. Help students, through his or her grading, to love learning

Key Points

Based on the aforementioned details, here are some important key points:

1. Teaching is an integral part of assessment and vice versa.
2. In teaching, assessment must be nondiscriminatory.
3. Teaching involves collaboration and consultation with parents in the assessment process.
4. Teaching is devalued when evaluation and grading are punitive.
5. Teaching and assessment must involve teamwork that functions ecologically.

Case 14

Ruthie was a Native American student who came from an upper-middle-class suburban home. She attended a "good" elementary school with her brother and sister, and they were consistently brought early to school by their parents. Ruthie was the only Native American in her class. The teacher documented rates of attendance and tardiness. In this school, students with 10 tardies were required to meet the principal. Even though Ruthie came early to school, the teacher failed to recognize this and documented seven tardies. When confronted by Ruthie's parents about the documentation, the teacher indicated, "The school bus came late seven times. I believe Ruthie comes to school daily with the bus." The parents were irritated and complained to the principal that the teacher had documented seven tardies for Ruthie, whereas her siblings, who were brought to school at the same time, had had no tardies documented by their teachers.

Traditional Problems and Solutions

In Case 14, there are apparent problems that include the following:

1. There was a negative perception of Ruthie in the class.
2. Ruthie's teacher seemed to have drawn an illusory conclusion about her.
3. Although it is true that documentation is important, Ruthie's teacher was more interested in documenting tardiness than in teaching.
4. Ruthie was made to feel like an "invisible" student in her class.
5. Ruthie's teacher believed in the myth of socioeconomic dissonance. The fact that Ruthie was a Native American did not make her disadvantaged socioeconomically.
6. There was some underlying prejudice on the part of Ruthie's teacher.
7. Ruthie's teacher saw what she wanted to see (i.e., Ruthie was a "poor" Native American student who came late daily). As a result, her learning environment became extremely restrictive for Ruthie.

Traditionally, many "good" teachers inappropriately document students' behaviors. Even though teachers are required to observe and document antecedent behaviors before designing Behavior Intervention Plans, their prejudice and belief systems can affect how they evaluate behaviors. The teacher in Case 14 believed that Ruthie came to school by bus, and because the bus was late seven times, she assumed that Ruthie was tardy seven times. Many "good" teachers fail to understand who their students are. Is it any wonder that many students confront teacher-generated stressors? Using the evaluation process inappropriately creates abundant problems. It is unfortunate that even supposedly "good" teachers see what they want to see. Rather than using documentation to see how students can be helped to maximize their potential, many "good" teachers use documentation punitively and almost senselessly.

Culturally Responsive Solutions

In Case 14, Ruthie was misevaluated by her teacher. She was made to feel like an invisible student in her class—her presence never caught the attention of her teacher. Based on Case 14, I believe a truly "good" teacher should do the following:

1. Document behaviors appropriately
2. Not have preconceived notions about any student
3. Dissociate him- or herself from the myth of socioeconomic dissonance
4. Know the *total* student
5. Talk with his or her students' parents
6. Learn to be very observant
7. Be culturally sensitive
8. Spend more time documenting how he or she can reach his or her students, and less time on how to document behaviors that do not exist
9. Document behaviors without malice
10. Apologize when he or she makes documentation mistakes

Key Points

Based on the aforementioned details, here are some important key points:

1. Teaching involves unprejudicial documentation.
2. Teaching involves the knowledge of students' and teachers' strengths.
3. Teaching, when properly done, involves the total student.
4. Teaching does not entail cultural and personal devaluing.

5. Teaching involves the power of observation, which is an integral part of assessment.

Strategic Lessons Learned

This chapter has acknowledged the importance of assessment (e.g., observation and documentation) in the instructional process. It is clear that assessment cannot be unidimensionally used to grade, promote, or punish students. It is important that "good" schools recruit and retain "good" teachers who understand the basic ingredients of assessment. What follows are assessment principles to which good teachers must adhere:

1. Assessment is a part of teaching, and teaching is a part of assessment.
2. Some degree of bias is inevitable in a country such as ours with diverse cultures, but we must strive for the least biased methods of assessment.
3. Proper assessment must respond to individual differences and use a variety of methods within one setting.
4. Our common goal must be to minimize the negative consequences of testing.
5. The ideal assessment tool may never be produced, but as inclusive classrooms become more widespread, we must take the responsibility to open our minds to new methods.
6. We must strive to maximize the potential of all students by providing appropriate assessment, intervention, and opportunities.
7. We can assist students in learning about their intellectual and academic abilities.
8. Traditional assessment techniques are narrow and unidimensional.
9. Parents must be taught the pros and cons of assessment.

10. When done wrong, assessments can lead to inappropriate labels, categories, expectations, placements, and teaching.

11. We must explore our own personally held views before assessing students from different cultural and socioeconomic backgrounds.

12. We together with parents must shift our paradigms regarding our views on how intelligence is assessed.

13. We should learn how our views on intelligence testing critically influence our classroom decisions.

14. General and special educators must be tolerant in order for assessment to work.

15. Everyone involved in the assessment process, including parents, should be aware of exactly what is being done for the student, problems with testing and interpretation of data, and problems of disproportionate placement and instruction.

4

❦————❦

Classroom Labels
and Categories

Labels and categories are a part of life. As human beings, we are identified by the labels we carry. Although labels and categories can be literally and simplistically explained as being just words, they have the power to classify, exalt, or humiliate. In William Shakespeare's *Julius Caesar*, the three conspirators used the power of words to convince the masses that they were right to kill Caesar as a potential dictator. This label, *dictator*, became the powerful word that turned the citizenry against Julius Caesar. Later, Marcus Antonius, one of Caesar's supporters, was given the opportunity to speak to the masses. He also used the power of words to convince the masses that Julius Caesar was a great leader who had no intention of becoming a dictator. A revolution ensued, and the whole nation was devastated.

Should we then legislate against words because of their power to humiliate people? Should we also legislate when they ought to be used? Labels (e.g., mental retardation, learning disability, speech and language impairment, physical and health impairment, behavior disorders, and gifted and talented) have been helpful in identifying specific problems confronting people. However, "sometimes, these labels stereotype potential capabilities" (Obiakor, 1996a, p. 77). Additionally, we have attached great power to words such as *White, Black, rich, poor, strong, lazy, good school, bad school, good kids, bad kids, smart,* and *dumb.* As I observed a few years ago,

> these words create more stereotypes than the problems they intend to solve. As we address the issues of inclusive education, we must revisit the power of words. Words are powerful, and the meanings we attach to them can be counterproductive to individuals using them and individuals receiving them. We have tended to use "magic" words to discuss simple situations. The critical question is, What words can bring us together as a community of peoples? (Obiakor, 1996a, p. 77)

Discussions of labels and categories have sometimes focused on political correctness rather than on the impact of such labels and categories. There is no doubt that words can be both beautiful and ugly. When they are beautiful, they inspire us to maximize our potential, but when they are ugly, they devalue our human character and create categories, labels, victims, and divisions. Reactions to the term *political correctness* have become a game that has tended to dissuade people from having warranted reactions to negative and hurtful labels. In these days of demographic shifts in paradigms and powers, our foci must be on encouraging words and labels that (a) increase tolerance and valuing of other people; (b) build people's accurate self-concepts; (c) inspire people to maximize their potential; (d) motivate people to become functional, goal-directed decision makers; and (e) empower people to appreciate the beauties of their human existence. These important points are the thrust of this chapter.

I am convinced that words and labels are powerful; because they are powerful, we must continue to use them not just to create or become victims but also to foster an esprit de corps in our communication, consultation, collaboration, and cooperation with others different from us (Duvall, 1994; Grossman, 1995; Obiakor, 1996b). In many "good" schools, teachers fail to understand the power of their words—they sometimes use them to victimize and label their innocent students. Lest we forget, Henry Rogers, in his classic book *Rogers' Rules for Success* (1984), advised us to do the following:

1. Think before we speak
2. Stop, look, listen, think, and feel!
3. Know our target audience
4. Think of the other person's needs and interests
5. Be sensitive to the individuals in the group when addressing the group
6. Keep communicating

When labels are inappropriately used and applied, they usually have far-reaching and devastating effects. Nicholas Hobbs, in his 1975 book *The Futures of Children: Categories, Labels, and Their Consequences,* understood that words and labels are needed to classify students, but he also agreed that they make victims out of students. As he pointed out,

1. Classification of exceptional children is essential to get services for them, to plan and organize helping programs, and to determine the outcomes of intervention efforts. (p. 5)

2. Public and private policies and priorities must manifest respect for the individuality of children and appreciation of the positive values of their individual talents and diverse cultural backgrounds. Classification procedures must not be used to violate this fundamental social value. (p. 6)

3. There is a growing public concern over the uses and abuses of categories and labels as applied to

children, and there is widespread dissatisfaction with inadequate, uncoordinated, and even hurtful services for children; we assume that all citizens share responsibility for these unsatisfactory circumstances as well as for their repair. (p. 8)

4. Special programs for "handicapped" children should be designed to encourage fullest possible participation in the usual experiences of childhood, in regular schooling and recreational activities, and in family and community life. When a child must be removed from normal activities, he should be removed the best possible distance, in time, in geographical space, and in the psychological texture of the experience provided. (p. 9)

5. Categories and labels are powerful instruments for social regulation and control, and they are often employed for obscure, covert, or hurtful purposes: to degrade people, to deny their access to opportunity, to exclude "undesirables" whose presence in some way offends, disturbs familiar custom, or demands extraordinary effort. (p. 11)

6. Categories and labels may open up opportunities for exceptional children, facilitate the passage of legislation in their interest, supply rallying points for volunteer organizations, and provide a rational structure for the administration of governmental programs. (p. 13)

7. Our nation provides inadequately for exceptional children for reasons linked to their being different; it also provides inadequately for exceptional children because it provides inadequately for all children. There is urgent need for a quickened national conscience and a new national policy with this as a goal: to nurture well all of our children, in body, mind and spirit, that we as a people may

grow in wisdom, strength, and humane concerns. (p. 14)

Hobbs (1975) concluded,

Classification of exceptional children is necessary at every level of organized concern for them. At the federal government, it is essential to have reasonably reliable estimates of the prevalence of problems as a basis for legislation and as a means of assessing the success or failure of national programs designed to help children. At the level of state governments, provisions must be made to fund specific services and to hold schools and other agencies accountable for carrying out prescribed programs. At the level of the school or agency, in classroom or clinic, what is done for a child depends on how his [her] problems are defined; that is, on how they are classified. Classification also serves certain political purposes: to appeal to legislators who have an interest in some particular "handicapping" condition, or to mobilize voluntary organizations. Is it too much to expect that any single classification system could serve such a range of purposes? Is there any way to classify children in order to get help for them without resorting to stigmatizing labels? (pp. 98-99)

Blackhurst and Berdine (1993) and Ysseldyke, Algozzine, and Thurlow (2000) agreed with Hobbs's (1975) statements when they reiterated the dangers of labels in students. According to Ysseldyke et al. (2000),

labeling students is not a benign activity nor is it a necessary evil, as school officers and others sometimes claim. Despite a presumed need for them, labels are an unfortunate by-product of a system that attaches money to acts, thus resulting in classifications and categories. Labels are often irrelevant to the instructional needs of students. Furthermore, labels become real attributes that prevent meaningful understanding of actual individual learning needs. By causing some to believe that students labeled as having mental retardation cannot perform certain tasks, the act of classifying condemns these students to a life of lesser expectations and performance. Labels require official sanction. Resources diverted to the process of identifying and classifying students are extensive. Time and money spent on labeling are time and money not spent on teaching. Time spent being labeled is time not spent on being taught or learning. (p. 110)

Based on the details discussed previously, the classroom teacher has an incredible opportunity to discover students' strengths and deficiencies. It is important for "good" teachers to be careful about the words and labels they use to classify students, especially when students come from culturally, linguistically, and socioeconomically diverse backgrounds. Additionally, it is important that good teachers learn the devastating effects of labels and classifications. Whereas labels lead to categories that are sometimes necessary to intervene when problems are apparent, when abused they create stigmas, stereotypes, and divisions that are unnecessary in this age of "full inclusion" and demographic shifts in paradigms and powers. The critical question is this: Should "good" schools not be cognizant of the devastating effects of labels in this new millennium? Consider the following pertinent cases.

Case 15

Chidi was a brilliant African American student who attended a "good" suburban school. His parents had recently moved to this suburb. As a new student, he began to adjust to his new peers. He happened to be the only African American in his class. As a rule, in this suburban school, students received weekly progress reports to acquaint parents of their children's progress. Chidi received the comment "He does not follow directions." This was a serious concern for

Chidi's parents—as a result, they spoke to their son about paying attention and following instructions. In the next couple of weeks, Chidi received similar comments that he "failed to follow directions." Because his parents were required to sign these weekly reports, they wanted to know from the teacher what she meant by those comments. Her comments were even more perplexing for Chidi's parents. She responded, "There is a way that Chidi does his face in class when instruction is taking place. His facial expression demonstrates a person with behavior problems." His parents pressed the teacher with further questions: "How can you label a student as a person who does not follow instructions based on facial expression and not based on how he or she performed in class?" "Have you talked with Chidi to see if he follows your classroom directions?" "Do you know Chidi's learning styles?" "If you know his learning styles, will you still label him as someone who does not follow directions?" The teacher responded, "Well, I just see his behavior as a problem. I have been teaching for many years."

Traditional Problems and Solutions

In Case 15, there are apparent problems that include the following:

1. The teacher failed to understand Chidi and how he learned.
2. The teacher's willingness to judge and label now and teach later was evident.
3. Chidi's presence as the only African American student constituted a problem for his teacher.
4. Chidi's teacher was obviously trying to label him based on his facial expression.
5. The teacher's inability to communicate with Chidi and his parents was a serious classroom impediment.
6. The focus on Chidi was not on his ability or inability to learn. It was on a behavior problem that never existed.

7. The teacher's efforts to make classroom directions and adjustments for Chidi (the new student) were not mentioned.

Traditionally, schools label students based on their scores on standardized norm-referenced tests. In many cases, teachers in "good" schools label their students when they do not like them, when they want to classify them, and when they want to get rid of them. Although the idea behind classroom labeling might be to prescribe pertinent instruction or intervention, many "good" students have been mislabeled and miscategorized by many "good" teachers. It is unfortunate that most students who get mislabeled and miscategorized are those who come from culturally, linguistically, and socioeconomically diverse backgrounds (Hobbs, 1975; Mercer, 1972, 1973; Obiakor, 1999a, 1999b, 1999c). Logically, when discriminatory tests that lack reliability and validity are used to assess these students, they produce discriminatory results, which include misidentifications, mislabelings, and miscategorizations.

Culturally Responsive Solutions

As stated, many "good" teachers in good schools mislabel and miscategorize their students, especially if the students speak, act, and learn differently. In Case 15, Chidi was mislabeled as a student who does not follow directions. Two critical questions surface here: Is there a difference between not understanding directions and not following them? What efforts were made by Chidi's teacher to make directions clearer and classroom adjustments smoother? The unfortunate thing about labels is that they create stigmas, lead to inaccurate self-evaluations, and establish unnecessary boundaries that do not harmonize learning environments. Based on Case 15, I believe a truly "good" teacher should do the following:

1. Not label or categorize his or her students
2. Be leery of labels

3. Teach on the basis of the student's strengths and weaknesses

4. Communicate with parents before labeling

5. Be careful about using labels to abuse students

6. Be cognizant of the devastating effects of labels

7. Know the difference between not following directions and not understanding directions

8. Not play God (e.g., using facial expressions to judge behavior problems)

9. Be knowledgeable about how to make his or her classroom environment conducive for learning

10. Understand that it takes some time to adjust to a new environment, peers, and teacher

Key Points

Based on the aforementioned details, here are some important key points:

1. Teaching involves labeling, but it also involves sensitivity and caring.

2. Teaching involves the manipulation of the learning environment, especially for new students.

3. Teaching does not involve prejudicial assumptions that in turn lead to labels.

4. Teaching involves self-concept enhancement.

5. Teaching involves communication with parents to reduce unnecessary labels.

Case 16

Maria was a Hispanic American student who attended a "good" school. She excelled in all her classes but spoke English with an accent. Her classmates ridiculed her consistently; however, she never wanted to tell her parents.

This young girl did not want to disappoint her parents. Her teacher rarely responded to the abuses she took in class. In fact, the teacher noted, "That's life, Maria. If you stay in this country, you'd better get used to such classroom activities." The teacher instead focused on how Maria held her pencil, how she wrote, and how she spoke. As a result, Maria was referred for testing without the help of the bilingual translator. This resulted in her being labeled "LD" (learning disabled). Maria did not know what LD meant, and she asked the resource room teacher, "They said I am LD. Does that mean that I am a 'Little Dumb'?" The experienced resource room teacher responded, "It does not mean that you are a little dumb; it just means that you learn differently." When Maria's parents asked her classroom teacher what "LD" meant to their daughter's education, she responded, "LD means that Maria will be spending more time with the resource room teacher because she has problems."

Traditional Problems and Solutions

In Case 16, there are apparent problems that include the following:

1. The teacher showed gross insensitivity toward Maria. Obviously, she had negative expectations of her.
2. Maria's linguistic difference was misinterpreted as weakness.
3. Maria was referred for testing that she did not really need.
4. Maria was labeled "LD," and even as a young girl she knew that something was wrong with that label.
5. The teacher succeeded in excluding Maria from regular instruction.
6. Maria endured some psychological and self-concept issues about which she never told her parents.
7. Maria was misidentified, misassessed, and miscategorized.

Traditionally, many "good" students who come from culturally and linguistically diverse backgrounds are mislabeled because of teacher expectations (see Obiakor, 1999a, 1999b, 1999c). Even "good" teachers in "good" schools fall into this trap. They find it difficult to deal with intraindividual and interindividual differences—they view differences as *deficits*. As a result, they mislabel and miscategorize students without recognizing their strengths and weaknesses. For instance, in Case 16, Maria excelled in her classes, yet she was ridiculed because of her cultural and linguistic differences. Public Law 94-142 (Education of All Handicapped Children's Act; later reauthorized as Public Law 101-476, Individuals With Disabilities Education Act) prescribed the use of the needed professional (e.g., the bilingual educator specialist) when testing students who have linguistic differences. The question continues to be this: Should "good" schools not be environments that allow all students to maximize their fullest potential?

Culturally Responsive Solutions

As indicated, many "good" teachers are insensitive to students who look, act, and speak differently. This insensitivity frequently results in abuses in test usage, identification, and categorization. In Case 16, Maria's classroom treatment by her peers was ignored. She was ridiculed and excluded from classroom activities, and her teacher discriminatorily referred her for testing, which resulted in a label of LD. Based on Case 16, I believe a truly "good" teacher should do the following:

1. Try to know his or her student
2. Respond to cultural and linguistic differences
3. Continue to change, or he or she will be consumed by change
4. Take the responsibility for the "good" and the "bad" in his or her class
5. Not look at his or her student from a deficit perspective
6. Highlight the multiple intelligences of his or her students

7. Positively manipulate his or her classroom environment
8. Not label or be a part of those who label his or her student
9. Value the "goodness" of his or her students
10. Work collaboratively and consultatively with parents to avoid prejudicial identifications, assessments, labels, and categories

Key Points

Based on the aforementioned details, here are some important key points:

1. Teaching incorporates the ecological experiences of students.
2. Teaching involves "quality with a heart."
3. Teaching, when done right, can help reduce student stressors.
4. Teaching involves valuing cultural, linguistic, and human differences.
5. Teaching, when improperly done, can have far-reaching, devastating effects on students, especially those who come from culturally, linguistically, and socioeconomically diverse backgrounds.

Case 17

Phil attended a well-known "good" school. He was an Asian American (specifically Hmong) student who performed very well in reading and writing but had a below-average performance in mathematics and sciences. Phil wanted to be a lawyer. Because he did not excel in the sciences, his teacher felt disappointed, which at some point resulted in a rage. On one occasion, his teacher called him a "dumb Asian" and recommended him for testing. Phil's parents were afraid to confront the school, and the teacher took advantage of the reserved culture of most Asians. Phil got so frustrated that he began to hate school and to hang out in the streets. Not long after that, he dropped out of school, was arrested for petty crimes, and was sent to a juvenile facility.

Traditional Problems and Solutions

In Case 17, there are apparent problems that include the following:

1. Phil's talents and areas of interest were downplayed.
2. Phil's teacher was surprised that Phil was not interested in mathematics and sciences.
3. Phil was labeled "dumb Asian" because he manifested unique differences.
4. Phil's learning environment was not conducive to his needs.
5. Phil's parents were intimidated by the teacher.
6. Phil's learning styles were ignored by the teacher.
7. Phil dropped out of school and got involved in crime.

Traditionally, even "good" teachers find it difficult to deal with "new" differences. There is a dangerous presumption that Asian Americans are only good in the sciences—this presumption goes hand in glove with the "model minority syndrome." Based on this syndrome, general and special educators do not expect Asian Americans to have problems in school. Because they have problems like other culturally and linguistically diverse learners, they need professionals who understand their circumstances and value their strengths and weaknesses in nondiscriminatory ways. In Case 17, Phil's teacher could not understand why he wanted to be a lawyer. The question here is this: Do we not need lawyers of all persuasions just as we need professionals of all persuasions? Because some teachers are viewed as "good," they think that they have all the answers and believe that things have to be in certain orders. As in Case 17, Phil's treatment at school encouraged him to drop out of school and enter into a world of crime. Such a negative consequence could have been prevented had the teacher respected Phil for the strengths he brought to school.

Culturally Responsive Solutions

As stated, many "good" teachers ignore the strengths and learning styles of their students. They seem to presume that they have prescribed solutions for all their students without recognizing the intraindividual and interindividual differences that students manifest. Many questions remain unanswered in the above situation. Phil's areas of interest were downplayed, and his self-worth was threatened. The silence of his parents was misconstrued. This is an obvious problem of the model minority syndrome. Based on Case 17, I believe a truly good teacher should do the following:

1. Have wisdom and common sense and, most of all, exercise them
2. Not be bogged down by the model minority syndrome
3. Be interested in building accurate self-knowledge, self-esteem, and self-ideals
4. Be a good person
5. Never label his or her students
6. Have some "soul"
7. Communicate with his or her students' parents
8. Be concerned when his or her student drops out of school
9. Be open-minded
10. Respond to human differences and learning styles

Key Points

Based on the aforementioned details, here are some important key points:

1. Teaching involves sensitivity and caring.
2. Teaching involves the recognition of students' strengths and energies.
3. Teaching, when done right, responds to human differences and dynamics.
4. Teaching has positive or negative consequences.
5. Teaching, when done right, reduces unrealistic expectations and illusory generalizations.

Case 18

Don is a Native American student who attended a "good" preschool program. Even though this program had the reputation of preparing students for the future, it also had the reputation of insensitivity toward minority children and their parents. On one occasion, Don's parents came to pick him up and saw him crying intensely. When his parents asked why he was crying, the preschool teacher indicated, "He was rude." They wanted to know what she meant by "rude," and she stated, "I have been doing this job for years. Most minority children are 'rude' because they come from disadvantaged environments." Don's parents were irate regarding this description of their son because they did not feel that they came from disadvantaged environments. So, they pushed further to know why their son was crying, and the preschool teacher responded, "We gave him a time-out because he was playing with toys when he was not supposed to." Don's parents wanted to know why their son was given a time-out without their consent. Sadly, the preschool teacher could not understand why Don's parents objected to her punishing their son, and she finally noted, "Well, your son has behavior disorders. We want to begin early to nip them in the bud."

Traditional Problems and Solutions

In Case 18, there are apparent problems that include the following:

1. The teacher misperceived Don as a child who came from a disadvantaged environment.
2. The teacher forgot that Don is a young child who needs caring guidance.
3. Don's parents were misjudged.
4. There appeared to be a conflict created by the teacher's behavior toward Don's parents.
5. The teacher labeled Don a "rude" child with behavior disorders.
6. Don's learning environment appeared unconducive to his needs.
7. The teacher's insensitivity was obvious.

Traditionally, many "good" teachers assume that all culturally and linguistically diverse learners come from disadvantaged backgrounds. There is an underlying presumption that these students come to school with negative packages of behavior—this deficit perspective downplays the strengths that students bring to school, as happened in Case 18, where Don was viewed as a student with a disordered behavior. By law, before a behavior is viewed as a disordered behavior it has to (a) depart from accepted standards considering age, sex, culture, situation, and circumstance; (b) be well-documented in its frequency; and (c) be well-documented in its duration. In addition, the presumption that all culturally and linguistically diverse students are "rude" is a prejudicial expectation that frequently leads to illusory conclusions.

Culturally Responsive Solutions

As indicated, many "good" teachers tend to ignore the cultural backgrounds of their students. As a result, they find themselves in conflicts with their students and parents. Early intervention is good, but early labeling or categorization has devastating effects. Many a time, in an attempt to "flog the devil" out of students, we tend to "put the devil" into them. It is educationally destructive for young children to start early to experience racist and heartless teachers. As in Case 18, Don's age, culture, and circumstance were not considered in the process. The teacher sadly assumed that he had problems that needed to be dealt with. Based on Case 18, I believe a truly "good" teacher should do the following:

1. Avoid indiscriminate labeling of students
2. Treat all his or her students with respect
3. Not look at his or her students from a deficit perspective
4. Not assume that his or her students have behavior disorders before testing them
5. Be knowledgeable about categories of exceptionalities to avoid miscategorization
6. Value his or her students' cultural and racial backgrounds
7. Be leery of labels because they create illusory generalizations
8. Teach with a "heart"
9. Know that early labels create early stigmas
10. Collaborate and consult with parents and community members

Key Points

Based on the aforementioned details, here are some important key points:

1. Teaching involves cultural and human valuing.
2. Teaching, when done right, creates opportunities for teachers and parents to work as partners.
3. Teaching involves realistic expectations.
4. Teaching involves documentation, not gut feelings.

5. Teaching, when done right, creates environments where students, teachers, and parents maximize their potential.

Strategic Lessons Learned

This chapter has discussed the intricacies involved in labeling and categories. It acknowledges the power of words and why we should use them carefully. It appears that "good" schools, "good" programs, and even "good" teachers are trapped by labels. My argument is that "good" schools ought to be places where good teachers are leery of labeling and categorizing students indiscriminately or discriminatorily. What follows are important principles for "good" teachers:

1. Because words have power, they must be used to empower students.
2. Race matters in labels and categories.
3. Parents must be empowered as equal partners to reduce the effects of labels and categories.
4. It is better to document behaviors than to use gut feelings.
5. Children and youths are best served when programs emphasize services needed and not types or labels of children.
6. If a categorical label is absolutely needed, it should be used to identify the specific problem and not the child.
7. No child or youth is a disordered child or youth.
8. Behaviors are "good" or "bad" depending on the culture, age, gender, time, and circumstance.
9. Negative behaviors of teachers have far-reaching consequences.
10. Individual differences in students must be valued to reduce labels and categories.
11. When students' differences are loaded with deficit perspectives, good students and good teachers fail.

12. "Good" labels can open educational doors for children, and "bad" labels can close those same doors.
13. Education should build trusts and not destroy them.
14. Inappropriate identifications lead to inappropriate assessments, which in turn lead to inappropriate labels.
15. All students are exceptional—they can learn when we provide nondiscriminatory labels, remediating services, and conducive learning environments.

5

Classroom
Placements
and Inclusions

The mentality in our "good" schools and society is "three strikes and you're out." As a result, many of our children and youths are indiscriminately suspended and expelled without due process proceedings. As an example, in many states in the United States, minorities make up the majority of the prison populations—in fact, there are more of them in jails than in colleges. From my perspective, there is something sadly puritanical about this picture—it fails to acknowledge our schools' and society's incapability to deal with cultural, socioeconomic, and situational differences. In schools, there are different forms of placement options (e.g., the regular classroom, the resource room, the self-contained classroom, the alternative classroom, the institution, and the inclusive classroom). These placement options determine the kinds of

instruction, intervention, and treatment that individuals receive. The challenge, however, is how students can be included
or excluded from educational programs in order to succeed in
least restrictive environments. The questions are these: Can
general and special educators maximize the potential of their
students in placements that are culturally, linguistically, racially, and socioeconomically restrictive? How "good" are
schools when they get rid of their students who do not fit into
the norms? These questions remain critical as we redefine
"good" schools and challenge practitioners to respond to demographic shifts in paradigms and powers (Obiakor, 2000b;
Ysseldyke et al., 2000).

The reasons for restrictive classroom placements of culturally and linguistically diverse (CLD) students are not divorced from inappropriate identifications, assessments, and
categories. Sadly, there are sociocultural, sociopolitical, and
sociohistorical contexts involved. As Artiles (1998) succinctly
put it,

The deficit view of minority people might often mediate
White people's cognitive, emotional, and behavioral reactions to minority individuals, phenotypes, interactive
styles, language proficiency, and world views. This is
probably why, for instance, a police officer in Miami
stops a Black man when driving in a predominantly White
neighborhood, or why a security person in a department
store in Virginia closely monitors a Black woman. This
might also explain why a Chicano man in Los Angeles
could not obtain a passport because he did not persuade
the Immigration and Naturalization Service that he was
born in the United States even after providing them with
the required documentation, or why people in Seattle
speak louder or slower to a Latino who speaks with an
accent. Indeed, these are routine events in the daily lives
of minority people. . . . We need to acknowledge, therefore, that human difference has been seen as problematic
in our society, that ethnic minority groups have been

traditionally seen as "problem people," and that discrimination, prejudice, and racism are subtly and openly
enacted every day in our country. (p. 33)

In our "good" schools, so many teachers and administrators
have not been honest with themselves about their perceptions
of *differences.* They tend to rationalize and pretend that "all is
well." In reality, we know that "all is not well" with regard to
discussions on *race* and *culture.* For us to solve problems, we
must acknowledge that we have problems and that we intend
to do something about them. We must also understand the
connection between misidentification, misreferral, misassessment, miscategorization, and misplacement. There are causes
and effects of the disproportionate placement of CLD students
in special education and gifted programs. There must be
some unrealistic reasons for placing fewer CLD students in
gifted programs and more of them in special education programs, especially in programs for students with behavior
disorders. According to Patton (1998),

> In spite of the presence of convincing data on the over-
> representation issue and the extant literature challenging
> special education processes that lead to identification
> and placement, this problem continues to persist. Its per-
> sistence will continue unless we reanalyze old premises
> and reconstruct new premises underlying the field of
> special education. (p. 26)

Placement-related controversies have been prevalent in
today's "good" schools because of the link between placement
and intervention. Ysseldyke et al. (2000) argued,

> Simply placing students in classes or programs for stu-
> dents with disabilities is not enough; schools must ensure
> that the instruction delivered is appropriate to the needs
> of each learner. It must be provided in the least restric-
> tive environment (LRE) possible. (p. 122)

They added,

> Perhaps the first question that can be asked is, can a heterogeneous group of students, some with serious problems, be taught effectively in general education classrooms given existing instructional resources? Related issues concern the conditions in which such populations can be taught and the limits of accommodation, both with and without additional instructional resources or more powerful interventions. On a social level, issues remain about the effect that students with and without disabilities have on each other in the same classroom. Indeed, whether students with disabilities prefer integrated or segregated placements remains a fundamental, yet unanswered, question. (p. 128)

In many "good" schools, teachers, parents, and service providers strive to place students in programs for students with gifts and talents. There is a prevalent "feel good" mentality when students and placed in gifted programs. Schools are happy because their "good" students perform exceptionally well on standardized, norm-referenced tests. Parents are happy because they view themselves as *gifted parents* who have *gifted* kids. Teachers are happy because they view themselves as *gifted teachers*. The danger of this "gifted" phenomenon is that students are placed in exclusive programs that focus on only academics and not on emotional intelligence. In addition, there is an underlying perfectionist mentality that ignores students' imperfections and stages of human development. The society celebrates perfections and decries imperfections, yet life's realities are full of both perfections and imperfections. The tendency is to have high expectations, but this can create unnecessary competition that can be self-destructive to students, their peers, teachers, and parents. Ysseldyke et al. (2000) acknowledged that

> placement issues have a broader base than just those individuals with disabilities. The jump from special

education segregation to teaching (or grouping) students by their implied level is not a huge leap, and the effects of tracking have been noted repeatedly. (p. 135)

Not long ago, Pool and Page (1995) decried teaching via tracking when they wrote,

Teaching promotes "dumbed-down," skill-drill, ditto-drive, application-deficient curricula. It contributes to the destruction of students' dreams and the production of low student self-esteem. . . . These placements can start as early as six weeks into kindergarten; and even though placements supposedly are flexible, they generally are permanent. (p. 1)

From the aforementioned details, it is crystal clear that placements are important because of their relationship to intervention. Interestingly, this relationship can have devastating effects, especially when it results in unrealistic expectations of students by their teachers. Kauffman and Ford (1998) addressed the relationship between categories, labels, and placements in school programs. Other scholars and educators (e.g., Artiles, 1998; Ford, 1998; Patton, 1998; Valles, 1998) agreed that CLD students are disproportionately placed in special education and gifted programs. Not many of these students are placed in gifted programs, yet many of them are placed in special education programs. In Ford's (1998) confirmation of this practice, she explained that

regardless of the definition adopted, many states have designated arbitrary cutoff scores on achievement and intelligence tests. For example, in some states gifted students must have an IQ of 130 or higher; some states require achievement test scores at the 95th percentile or higher; in other states, students must score at or above the 98th percentile. Further, some states identify the highest 3% of the student population; other states identify 5%. Some states require schools to use four sources or types of information during decision-making process; others require five sources or types of information. Thus, a student can be identified as gifted in one state (or even neighboring school district), but not another based upon the definition adopted. Further, when and how that student is screened, identified, and served varies from one school district to another. (p. 8)

Rather than considering only the narrow perspective indicated by Ford (1998), educators making placements of CLD students should base gifted program placements on multidimensional perspectives. Ford correctly noted that "no one piece of information should be used to include or exclude a student from placement" (p. 11). A few years ago, Wechsler (1991) urged general and special educators to consider multiple factors in students' assessment and accountability processes. As he pointed out,

it cannot be presumed that the array of tasks, standardized and presented as the WISC-III [Wechsler Intelligence Scale for Children III] can cover all of an individual's intelligence—other determiners of intelligence, nonintellective in nature, also help shape how a child's abilities are expressed. These nonintellective factors—include attributes such as planning and goal awareness, enthusiasm, attitudes, field dependence and independence, impulsiveness, anxiety, and persistence. . . . [We] must consider an individual's life history (e.g., social and medical history and linguistic and cultural background) as part of any good assessment. . . . [It is] important to take into account factors other than intellectual or cognitive abilities. (pp. 2-3)

As we redefine "good" schools and reassess how teachers in these schools teach, we must be aware of problems associated with classroom placements of *all* students. "Good" schools should be environments where students' cultures and languages do not result in misidentification, misassessment, miscategorization, and misplacement. We must look at the total picture! In the words of Kea and Utley (1998), "to teach me is to know me" (p. 44). We cannot pretend that race does not matter in our perceptions of students—we cannot also pretend that we do not see colors or hear languages. Valles (1998) summarized that "if teachers are going to work in classrooms with more diverse groups, now and in the future, it would seem apparent that culturally and linguistically appropriate methods and materials should be an emphasis of preservice training" (p. 53). Also important in Valles's contexts are inservice trainings that might bring together general and special education professionals to see how systematic support mechanisms could be instituted. Whether or not full inclusion is an illusion (Kauffman & Hallahan, 1995), the heart and soul of teachers must be in teaching to infuse quality and equity in nonrestrictive placements and settings. The fact remains that full inclusion creates opportunities for all students to be taught through collaborative endeavors of professionals. In its on-line booklet *Improving Education: The Promise of Inclusive Schools,* the National Institute for Urban School Improvement (2000) concluded,

Inclusive schooling practices embrace the idea that since everyone is an individual, we need to organize schools, teaching, and learning so that each student gets a learning experience that "fits." Our past separate system of special education taught us that we could provide individual attention when it was needed.

Schools of the future need to ensure that each student receives the individual attention, learning accommodations, and supports that will result in meaningful learning to high standards of achievement. In fact, our schools need to be inclusive schools using inclusive schooling practices.

Because inappropriate placements do not occur in isolation, it is imperative that good teachers understand how they are related to inappropriate identifications, assessments, labels, categories, and instructions-interventions. As a consequence, the following questions deserve some answers:

1. Should "good" schools not be where reliable and valid assessment tools are used to place students?
2. Should "good" schools not be where multiple sources are used to gather information about students before placements?
3. Should "good" schools not be where all students are provided with equitable support services and educational avenues for growth and development?
4. Should "good" schools not be where inservice opportunities are provided for teachers?
5. Should "good" schools not be where students are placed in nonrestrictive settings that help maximize their fullest potential?
6. Should "good" schools not be where teachers have the courage to inclusively teach?
7. Should "good" schools not be where placements are not based on a puritanical, perfectionist mentality?
8. Should "good" schools not be where placements are developmentally oriented?
9. Should "good" schools not be where full inclusion is not an illusion?
10. Should "good" schools not be where differences do not lead to biased placements?

Responding to these questions is critical to defining "good" schools. Times are changing, and our paradigms and powers must shift with the times. *Full inclusion ought to be the goal today and in the future.* Truly "good" teachers can reduce school failures and make full inclusion plausible (Lovitt, 2000; Ysseldyke et al., 2000). It is not impossible for *all* students to be educated in nonrestrictive environments as long as the unique needs of students are met (Smith, 1998; Wisconsin Department of Public Instruction, 2000). In fact, the least restrictive environment (LRE) provides opportunities for students' academic, social, and emotional developments. As Smith (1998) stated not long ago,

> LRE is an important concept. Special [and all] educators must be constantly aware of how placement decisions can segregate students by removing them from normal role models, social interactions, and curriculum—and can fragment their daily lives. Placement decisions further identify a student as being different. Finally, removing a child from the general education classroom has serious implications for today and the future. If, however, the student's needs cannot be met in the general classroom or if that environment impedes learning, then placement there is not appropriate. (p. 60)

Whether a student is misplaced in a gifted program or special education program, the effects can be devastating. These two placement options frequently result in unrealistic expectations, prejudicial generalizations, illusory conclusions, and deceptive self-aggrandizement. Should "good" schools not be where *all* students are appropriately placed in nonrestrictive environments that help maximize their potential? Consider the following pertinent cases.

Case 19

Carolyn was an African American student who attended a popular "good" school. She was a brilliant and creative student who liked tattoos and piercings. In this school, students were permitted to color their hair. On one occasion, Carolyn, one of the few African American students in this school, decided to emulate others who had permanently colored their hair. For this, Carolyn was asked to leave the class by her teacher. She wanted to know why she was singled out, and her teacher reported her to the principal. In no time, Carolyn was called into the principal's office to go and wash off her hair color. She refused, arguing that other students colored their hair also. When she refused, the principal called her parent. Her parent arrived and wanted to know why her daughter would be sent home. The principal responded, "We have a policy of people not temporarily coloring their hair. If your daughter wants to maintain this hair color, it's okay. If not, it's not okay." Carolyn's mother was perplexed and wanted to know why it was okay to permanently color hair and not okay to temporarily color hair. The principal responded, "Your daughter has tattoos. She looks like a troublemaker. As a result, I have recommended that she be placed in the 'alternative' school." Carolyn's parent decided to fight this placement through a lawsuit. Carolyn's school performance was affected even when the case was resolved. No teacher wanted her back, and she continued her education in the alternative school.

Traditional Problems and Solutions

In Case 19, there are apparent problems that include the following:

1. There appeared to be inconsistencies in how students were punished in the school (e.g., permanent hair coloring was allowed, but temporary hair coloring was not allowed).

2. The school was divorcing itself from what took place in the society (e.g., many adults pierce their ears and other places, many adults have tattoos, and many of them color their hair).

3. The principal and Carolyn's parent could not resolve their misunderstanding peacefully.

4. The principal attempted to disempower Carolyn and her parent.

5. Carolyn was placed in an "alternative" school for students with behavior problems.

6. Carolyn's educational success was affected.

7. Carolyn was not wanted by any of her teachers even when the issue was resolved—she had already been labeled, stigmatized, and placed.

Traditionally, in many "good" schools, the zero tolerance policy is not usually a reality. This policy frequently discriminates—there appears to be the policy that says "If we like you or if you come from the right race, it's okay. However, if we do not like you or if you do not come from the right race or culture, it's not okay." The policy of allowing students to permanently color their hair and disallowing them to temporarily color their hair demonstrates gross inconsistencies present in today's "good" schools. There are major problems associated with disproportionate placements of CLD students in *behavior disorders* programs. These students are unnecessarily stigmatized and labeled, and when they are placed nobody wants them back in regular classroom programs, and as a result, their education suffers. Additionally, when parents and students feel disempowered, collaboration, consultation, and cooperation in school activities are affected (Lovitt, 2000; Obiakor, 1996a). Rather than create crises, the role of a good school should be to manage crises (Obiakor, Darling, et al., 2000; Obiakor et al., 1997).

Culturally Responsive Solutions

Case 19 presents an African American student who attended a "good" school. According to the principal's remark, in this school, students were permitted to color their hair permanently but not temporarily. Of course, the rationale was unclear, and this forced the parent to take legal action. This legal action (even though it was resolved) did not ameliorate the far-reaching consequences of the "alternative program" placement. Based on Case 19, I believe a truly "good" teacher should do the following:

1. Not single out any one student for a mistake that everyone makes

2. Be consistent in his or her rules and regulations
3. Spend time teaching
4. Manage crises and not create them
5. Work collaboratively and consultatively with parents
6. Not "get rid of" his or her students
7. Not be a part of a conspiracy to get rid of his or her students
8. Consider the age, gender, and culture of a student before making placement suggestions
9. Care for his or her students at all times
10. Build self-concepts

Key Points

Based on the aforementioned details, here are some important key points:

1. Teaching involves collaboration and consultation.
2. Teaching, when done right, solves problems.
3. Teaching, when inappropriately done, can place students in restrictive environments.
4. Teaching is the uniting force between school and family.
5. Teaching, when done right, responds to individual differences.

Case 20

José was a Hispanic American student who attended a "good" school. He was an above-average and hard-working student. But because of his linguistic difference (i.e., he spoke with an accent), his classmates thought that he was not intelligent. José's parents came to school to complain about the restrictive nature of his learning environment. Surprisingly, the teacher and principal recommended that José be placed in a self-contained special education program to allow him to master English. José and his parents felt helpless and devastated by this placement option. They thought about suing the school but changed their minds because of financial constraints.

Traditional Problems and Solutions

In Case 20, there are apparent problems that include the following:

1. There appeared to be a clear misdefinition of what a "good" school is.
2. José's linguistic difference was misconstrued as a lack of intelligence.
3. There was a "cultural disconnect" in the classroom between the teacher and José and between classmates and José.
4. The learning environment was severely restrictive for José.
5. José's and his parents' due process rights were violated.
6. José and his parents felt helpless and devastated about the placement options.
7. Collaboration and consultation between José's parents and the school were damaged.

Traditionally, students from different cultural, linguistic, and socioeconomic backgrounds fail to maximize their fullest potential in school programs. Their culture and language are frequently viewed as deficits rather than as strengths. In addition, their learning styles are inhibited. As in Case 20, José and his parents were never acknowledged and respected in educational programming. *Language is an integral part of culture,* yet its deviation from what is spoken in a community is threatening. Ironically, the good school is supposed to enhance the learning process of the student (Obiakor, 1994, 2000b). Education should have the power to develop potential; however, in Case 20, it disempowered José and his parents. A house divided can never stand—the teacher, principal, and parents should have worked as equal partners in Case 20. It should be known that the more powerless parents are, the less cooperative they become.

Culturally Responsive Solutions

Case 20 exposes a typical scenario in today's "good" schools. Quality and equity must go together to reach students who learn, speak, and act differently. Difference is not a deficit—it should strengthen educational programming. Placing students in special education programs because of their cultural and linguistic differences is a dangerous disease that affects many "good" schools. Based on Case 20, I believe a truly good teacher should do the following:

1. Value the student's culture
2. View a student's language as his or her strength
3. View difference from a developmental perspective
4. Not misplace students
5. Be an advocate for his or her students
6. Believe in "quality with a heart"
7. Be sensitive and caring at all times
8. Have the courage to teach multidimensionally
9. Celebrate differences through *quality* education
10. Collaborate and consult with parents as equal partners

Key Points

Based on the aforementioned details, here are some important key points:

1. Teaching involves knowing who you are.
2. Teaching involves learning the facts when you are in doubt.

3. Teaching involves changing your thinking, especially when it is antiprogress.
4. Teaching involves building self-concepts.
5. Teaching, when done right, uses resource persons (e.g., parents and community members) to enhance learning.

Case 21

Kim was an Asian American student who was truly having problems in school. She was abusive to her peers and not doing well in her classes. In her "good" school, there was the presumption that all Asian Americans were great students. As a result, her teacher did not want her to be tested and placed in special education or alternative programs. Kim's parents thought she needed to see a counselor, and the teacher refused, indicating, "Asian Americans do not have learning or behavioral problems. They are 'smart' minorities who do not need counselors to survive." Kim continued to be exceedingly disruptive, and her teacher never responded. On one occasion, Kim took a knife and stabbed one of her classmates in the hand. It was only then that the school responded and placed her in an "alternative" program where she began to receive counseling.

Traditional Problems and Solutions

In Case 21, there are apparent problems that include the following:

1. Kim had learning and behavior problems that were downplayed by her teacher.
2. Even though Kim's behaviors deviated from the norm, she was still viewed as a "model" minority.
3. Kim was viewed from a unidimensional perspective (i.e., "smart minority syndrome").

4. Kim's emotional intelligence appeared not to matter, even though she continued to be abusive to her peers.
5. Students' stressors were downplayed—an early diagnosis would have been helpful.
6. Preventive measures were not taken to help Kim in school.
7. Kim's parents' request was ignored by the teacher.

Traditionally, many Asian Americans suffer in school programs because of the "model minority syndrome." They endure tremendous psychological problems, especially when they do not act as predicted by practitioners. In Case 21, Kim's mother was crying for help, but she was ignored. Why did the teacher fail to support the parents' suggestions of sending Kim to the counselor? Some teachers tend to think that they know their students more than the parents of those students do. As a result, Kim's emotional intelligence was downplayed. It is necessary that teachers understand the need to educate the total child (i.e., to build the academic, intellectual, social, physical, and emotional capabilities of students; see Obiakor, Darling, et al., 2000; Obiakor et al., 1997.

Culturally Responsive Solutions

Case 21 reveals typical problems that Asian Americans experience. These problems downplay their socioemotional well-being. *All* students need to be valued, in spite of their abilities or disabilities. Based on Case 21, I believe a truly "good" teacher should do the following:

1. Actively listen to the parents of his or her students
2. Prevent problems before they blow out of proportion
3. Resist the temptation of the model minority syndrome
4. Focus on educating the whole child
5. Manage student stressors
6. Teach, test, reteach, and retest as needed by his or her students

7. Collaborate with the multidisciplinary team (e.g., counselors, psychologists, teachers, administrators, parents, and students)
8. Educate students in the least restrictive environments
9. Know when to include or exclude students from the classroom
10. Divorce oneself from perceptual and illusory generalizations

Key Points

Based on the aforementioned details, here are some important key points:

1. Teaching involves active listening.
2. Teaching, when done right, reduces presumptions about people.
3. Teaching, when inappropriately done, downplays emotional intelligence.
4. Teaching helps to ameliorate stressors.
5. Teaching involves collaboration and consultation with the multidisciplinary team, including the parents.

Case 22

Jill was an above-average student who attended a "good" school. She was a Native American student; however, it was difficult to tell because of her physical features. Initially, she got along with her classmates, and everything was all right. In the social studies class, her teacher mentioned that "the Indians were primitive, nasty people who were saved by Whites." Jill did not appreciate this remark and told her parents. They came to school to tell the teacher to desist from making such untrue remarks that were prejudicially based. The teacher responded, "I didn't know that Jill is a Native American. She does not look like one." Surprisingly, Jill, who initially got along with her peers, began to have problems with them and her teacher. She was labeled a "troublemaker" and placed in a self-contained classroom for students with behavior disorders. Jill's teacher and parents began to have unresolved problems, and Jill's school performance dropped. When confronted, the school principal indicated that the self-contained placement would be better for Jill's emotional well-being. What an amazing turnaround from getting along to not getting along in school!

Traditional Problems and Solutions

In Case 22, there are apparent problems that include the following:

1. Jill went from a student who got along to someone who never got along in the classroom.
2. Jill's teacher exhibited the classic ignorance in today's schools.
3. Jill was labeled a "troublemaker" because she pointed out her teacher's racist statement.
4. Jill was placed in a self-contained classroom without testing or due process procedures.
5. Jill's school became a very restrictive environment for her.
6. Jill's cultural values were not respected by the teacher and the principal.
7. Collaboration and consultation with Jill's parents did not exist.

Traditionally, even "good" teachers do not know they can be prejudiced. Something is wrong when a student is labeled and placed in a program for his or her supposed well-being without assessment and due process procedures. First, it is against the law to do that. Second, it fails to respond to the unique needs of the student. Third, it is prejudicial. (In fact, in the case of Jill, it was racist.) And fourth, it demonstrates gross disrespect and insensitivity. Good schools should be where students maximize their fullest potential and where students' cultural values are not denigrated. In Case 22, the reverse was the situation—the prejudice was blunt, shameful, and devastating. The teacher's misinformation was challenged, and her solution was to label and "get rid of" the student (Obiakor, 1994; Obiakor & Algozzine, 1995).

Culturally Responsive Solutions

Case 22 exposes the "invisibility" that the status quo expects of culture. When culture is viewed as a deficit, the sacred existence of students in a classroom is threatened. Culture and race should be the embodiments of strength in a healthy learning environment. Based on Case 22, I believe a truly good teacher should do the following:

1. Know the power of words
2. Respect his or her students' cultural values
3. Not have a mental block—he or she should be open-minded
4. Not misplace his or her student
5. Have "soul"
6. Work collaboratively and consultatively with parents
7. Build self-concepts
8. Treat his or her students' parents as equal partners
9. Value the unique differences that his or her students bring to class
10. Have realistic expectations of his or her students and parents

Key Points

Based on the aforementioned details, here are some important key points:

1. Teaching involves respect for individual differences.
2. Teaching involves cultural and racial valuing.
3. Teaching can build self-concepts, and when poorly done, it can destroy self-concepts.
4. Teaching involves collaboration and consultation.
5. Teaching involves active listening and empathic inter-action in least restrictive environments.

Strategic Lessons Learned

This chapter has discussed issues and problems associated with disproportionate placements, inclusions, and exclusions. It explains, in detail, the least restrictive phenomenon (i.e., placements can be restrictive or nonrestrictive, depending on how they are done). My premise is that "good" schools ought to be where students are not disproportionately placed because of the color of their skin, linguistic differences, and racial identities. In addition, "good" schools should focus on how to help maximize the fullest potential of their students by building self-concepts. What follows are important principles for "good" teachers:

1. Race and culture matter in the placement of students.
2. Placements must be based on students' needs and not on racial and cultural identities.
3. Language difference should never be misconstrued as a lack of intelligence.
4. Empathy is an important ingredient of "good" teaching.
5. Inappropriate assessments lead to inappropriate labels and placements.
6. How a student is placed depicts how much value we place on him or her.
7. "Good" placements are least restrictive environments.
8. We "put the devil" in students when we try so hard to "flog the devil" out of them.

9. Differences are not deficits.

10. When we are in doubt, we must learn the facts.

11. Prejudicial placements have devastating effects on students.

12. We and our students' parents must collaborate and consult with each other.

13. Students are best served when their due process rights are respected.

14. All students have gifts and talents—education must have the power to tap human strengths and energies.

15. Full inclusion reduces biased exclusion of students in classroom activities.

6

Classroom Instructions and Interventions

"Good" identifications, referrals, assessments, account-abilities, labels, categories, placements, and inclusions are all basic ingredients of "good" instructions and interventions. In other words, *fraudulent* identifications and referrals result in *fraudulent* assessments and accountabilities, *fraudulent* labels and categories, *fraudulent* placements and inclusions, and *fraudulent* instructions and interventions. Only truly "good" teachers or interventionists have the power to shift traditional paradigms. Put another way, truly "good" teachers have the wherewithal to discover prejudicial loopholes in *all* components of classroom and school activities.

"Good" teachers are different! They believe in democracy and justice. In addition, they frequently experiment, learn, create, and implement. They love their profession and honor the tradition of their profession, but *they are progressive!* They are neither retrogressive traditionalists nor radical anarchists.

They are dynamic and abreast of the times. From my perspective, they are *progressive traditionalists* (i.e., they love and respect the tradition of their profession, yet they are innovative in how problems can be solved). For example, to a retrogressive traditionalist, a student who is tardy or absent should be suspended or even expelled, but to a progressive traditionalist, we need to find out why that student is tardy or absent and we need to discover other methods to work on tardiness, absence, or school drop-out rates. Additionally, to a retrogressive traditionalist, *all* school problems of the student are family related. To a progressive traditionalist, school failures might be family related, teacher related, peer related, school related, community related, or government related. Progressive traditionalists are analytical problem-solving individuals who believe there is always "a light at the end of the tunnel." These individuals do not curse the darkness—they light the candles! In this chapter, I argue that "good" classroom instructions and interventions have the power to light the candles in *all* students.

Based on the traditional "good" school phenomenon, unnecessarily strict teachers are viewed as "good." Many of these teachers, by error or design, ruin or "kill" the spirits of students, especially those who act, talk, look, and learn differently. These teachers lose their cool when they are thrown "curve balls" by students. They stop learning new ideas and resist getting out of their comfort zones (see Obiakor, 1994, 1999a, 1999b, 1999c). The results of their actions are frequently devastating, especially when they are defended by their "good" principals and "good" school district administrators. When teachers fail to teach, students are turned off, parents are upset, and conflicts ensue. When parents and teachers fail to work together, collaboration and consultation fail, and the student's future is in ruins. The critical question is this: Why should students (even good ones) come to school to be ruined by poorly prepared or unprepared teachers?

"Good" teaching is not easy—it is painstaking. I do not believe the teaching profession is a dumping ground for ne'er-do-wells. *It is an honorable profession that is spiritually based.* Hoyle (1975) recognized this in his book *The Role of the Teacher,* arguing that

teachers face a common set of basic problems in the classroom, but the ways in which they seek to solve these vary
considerably. The leadership styles of teachers have
particular reference to their managerial roles, but teaching styles embrace more than this. (pp. 63-64)

He added,

The roles which teachers play in the classroom and the
teaching styles which they adopt are greatly varied.
Some teachers will have a much more limited repertoire
than others, and the teacher's role and behavior will be
determined by the nature of his [her] personality, his
[her] experiences, and the teaching situations in which
he [she] finds himself [herself]. If a teacher is unable to
match his [her] style to the situation, it is likely that he
[she] will be ineffective, unhappy or both. (p. 68)

Hoyle's (1975) classic thesis is that the teacher's role is uniquely
based on him- or herself as a human being who brings to the
class unique human experiences. Interestingly, these experiences must find ways to interact with the experiences of his or
her students and parents. Conflicts are inevitable in classroom activities; however, "good" teachers are able to manage
and learn from them. As a result, how the teacher views supposed human imperfections makes his or her job intriguing
or rewarding. For instance, if the teacher views culture, language, socioeconomics, and learning style as deficits, his or
her teaching is negatively oriented. However, if he or she
views these human attributes from a developmental perspective, his or her teaching is positively oriented. Thus, the philosophy and beliefs of the teacher affect how he or she works
with students, especially when they are culturally, racially,
linguistically, and socioeconomically different.

    Teaching is a craft! It is unfortunate that many supposedly
"good" teachers fail to master their craft. It seems reasonable
then that teachers look for students' energy rather than potential. As Kohl (1988) pointed out,

the craft of teaching has a number of aspects. It relates to the organization of content and the structuring of space and time, so that learning will be fostered. It requires an understanding of students' levels of sophistication and the modes of learning they are accustomed to using. But most centrally, the craft of teaching requires what can be called teaching sensibility. This sensibility develops over a career of teaching and has to do with knowing how to help students focus their energy on learning and growth. What I mean by energy is close to what is more usually referred to as student "potential," but it's not quite that. Potential, I suppose, refers to what can be instead of what actually is at a given moment. When teachers say a student is not "working up to potential," they mean that he [she] isn't accomplishing something he [she] should be. When students are described as having little or no potential, they are presumed to be incapable of learning things that more "gifted" students can. This conviction that there are clear levels and on what it is possible to achieve is exactly what good teachers resist. One cannot look into children's souls and see the extent and limits of their potential. Potential is not located in any part of the brain or in any organ. We don't know what people (ourselves included) could become, and any limit on expectations will become a limit on learning. That is why I choose to think of energy instead of potential. The model is fluid—energy flows, it can be expended or renewed, latent or acting, it can be transformed from one form or manifestation to another. It exists in all areas of life, the emotional and physical as well as the intellectual and artistic. All youngsters have this energy, and a substantial part of the craft of teaching consists of knowing how to tap into children's energy sources or removing impediments to their flow. (pp. 57-58)

Truly "good" teachers intervene before, during, and after conflicts in the classroom. They are great interventionists (e.g., therapists and counselors). As a result, in their teaching activities, they appreciate and understand cultural diversity, inspire confidence and hope in their students, demonstrate flexibility in their techniques, are empathetic in their verbal and nonverbal communications, respect their students' self-worth, show genuineness in their expressions, and demonstrate expertness in their knowledge (Obiakor & Schwenn, 1995). Earlier, Trotter (1993) specifically indicated that genuineness is "evidenced through supporting nonverbal and role behavior, congruence, spontaneity, openness, and self-disclosing" (p. 144). Truly "good" teachers should understand that behaviors and attitudes are culturally based. Examples of these include culturally related behaviors such as working cooperatively rather than competitively, unresponsiveness to structure, no eye contact, hidden feelings, "inappropriate" smiling, desiring immediate payoffs, suspicion of authority, giving up easily to demonstrate respect or modesty, and concern with the social environment (Correa & Tulbert, 1991; Westby & Rouse, 1985).

Because "good" teaching and intervention is tied to good identification, assessment, placement, and instruction, it is very important that I reiterate the following teacher beliefs, which should be the guiding principles of excellent pedagogy:

1. There is no perfect human being.
2. Human beings differ intraindividually and interindividually.
3. A person's environment contributes to his or her growth and development, and this environment can be positively manipulated.
4. Because of human differences, our assessment and intervention techniques *must* be multidimensional.
5. Behavior problems do not occur in isolation—they are based on our personal idiosyncrasies.
6. A problem behavior is not always a disordered behavior.

7. What is a disordered behavior to one teacher or professional might not be a disordered behavior to another teacher or professional.

8. A behavior is a disordered behavior when (a) it departs from acceptable standards considering age, culture, situation, circumstance, and time; (b) its frequency is *well documented*; and (c) its duration is *well documented*.

9. Even when a behavior is disordered, the person exhibiting that behavior is not disordered or disturbed.

10. Assessment and intervention techniques that work for one student might not work for another student.

11. Two testers/assessors/diagnosticians might test a single student and get different results.

12. The ways tests are *conducted* and *interpreted* can have far-reaching effects on learners.

13. We "put the devil" in students when we try so hard to "flog the devil" out of them—we create problem behaviors when we solve problems that do not exist (i.e., iatrogenic intervention).

14. Collaboration, consultation, and cooperation can make behavioral and academic assessment more meaningful to students, parents, and educators.

15. It takes a whole village to raise a child—this comprehensive support model incorporates the student, family, school, community, and government. No part of the village should be excluded in behavioral and academic assessment and intervention. (Obiakor, 1999c, pp. 49-50)

More than three decades ago, Henderson and Bibens (1970) identified similar tips for teaching *all* students. As they noted, "good" teachers must do the following:

1. Attempt to understand the feelings of the students and to empathize with them
2. See all children as worthy beings, even though they might disapprove of their behaviors
3. Believe that all students are educable
4. Try to understand the environmental handicaps that may negatively affect children, but do not stereotype them
5. Seek ways to reach and interest students
6. Set clear, fair rules for each class and be firm in holding to them
7. Accept differences in cultural conditions and individual behaviors without showing signs of shock or ridiculing pupils
8. Recognize individual and variant styles of learning, and try to adapt teaching methods to fit them
9. Identify and utilize the strengths in students
10. Give students precise and concrete rewards, and recognize the importance of each child's experiencing success (p. 126)

Henderson and Bibens (1970) observed that "teachers differ from one another in size, weight, shape, degree of attractiveness, and personality development" (p. 142). They concluded that although students are not concerned about these characteristics they worry about answers to the following poignant questions:

1. Is the teacher able to put his [her] students at ease?
2. Is the teacher's voice pleasant, or is it harsh and irritating to the listener?
3. Is the teacher positive in his [her] classroom techniques or does he [she] have a negative approach to teaching?

4. Is the teacher able to present material in an interesting and meaningful way so that he [she] holds the attention of his [her] students?
5. Is the teacher sincere with members of his [her] class?
6. Does the teacher's classroom bearing suggest that he [she] enjoys teaching, or does it appear that to him [her] teaching is just a job?
7. Does the teacher exhibit a sense of humor, or is the entire learning situation a dry and boring process?
8. Does the teacher have a real concern for all of his [her] students? Does he [she] appear to want to help each student in the learning activity?
9. Does the teacher know and understand the material he [she] teaches, or does he [she] attempt to bluff his [her] way by pretending to know more than he [she] actually does? (p. 143)

I have consistently indicated that a "good" teacher or interventionist must (a) know who he or she is, (b) learn the facts when in doubt, (c) change his or her thinking, (d) use resource persons, (e) build self-concepts, (f) teach with divergent techniques, (g) make the right choices, and (h) continue to learn (see Obiakor, 1994, 1999a). The intricacies and complexities of teaching require that we know who we are to be good teachers (i.e., we must know our strengths, weaknesses, likes, dislikes, culture, race, and national origin). Our knowledge of who we are helps us know who our students are, and we begin to recognize humans intrapersonally and interpersonally. We must educate ourselves, our colleagues, and our students about cultural and racial facts. We must also learn new techniques through preservice and inservice training. There must be a difference between "good" teachers and "Joe Sixpacks" out there. Rather than make assumptions about assessments, labels, and categories, it is important that we learn as much as we can because students' futures and lives are at stake. As teachers, the facts that we learn are useless unless they help us

to change our thinking. Therefore we must avoid generalizations, respect differences between people, desist from prejudicial judgments, be willing to change, be accepting of shifting
paradigms, listen to all students, create rewarding environments, and empower all students. Not only must teachers
change their thinking, they must use resource persons or
other experts. In other words, "good" teachers invite guests
to their classes, empower parents, work with other teachers
collaboratively and consultatively, encourage students to work
cooperatively, encourage positive relationships between
parents and professionals, invite minority members of *all*
backgrounds to the classroom, and initiate contacts with
neighboring schools.

One of the teacher's important jobs in the classroom is to
develop self-concepts in students. To a large extent, "good"
teachers reward positive behaviors and achievements with
praise and other forms of reinforcement, inspire students to
be self-instructed, challenge students' strengths by relying
less on standardized test scores, put students' failures in
classroom tasks into proper perspective, and help students
set realistic goals. The "good" teacher must teach or intervene
with divergent techniques. Put another way, he or she must
do the following:

1. Make clear and simple classroom rules with the help of
   students
2. Teach information that relates to students' lives and
   realities
3. Greet each student every morning
4. Ask and answer questions in a nonthreatening manner
5. Notice and respect individual differences as well as
   similarities
6. Make ethics a priority
7. Have high expectations for all students
8. Encourage students to assert their opinions
9. Use culturally and linguistically relevant curriculum
   materials and instructional strategies

   10. Use collaborative and consultative team approaches for learning and teaching

In addition, "good" teachers must make the right choices. As a consequence, they must do the following:

   1. Educate themselves about things they do not know
   2. Desist from making derogatory assumptions about culture, language, race, gender, and socioeconomic status
   3. Use creative ideas to develop community interactions
   4. Create an atmosphere that invites parents, students, and staff
   5. Put each individual student in a positive, fun learning environment
   6. Think before acting
   7. Take charge with a smile
   8. Be knowledgeable about different teaching models
   9. Be proud of the teaching profession
  10. Express thoughts about global worldview

I believe "good" teachers must continue to learn innovative methods to reach their students. Also, they must continue to master their subject matter and craft. To a large measure, "good" teachers do the following:

   1. Become good students
   2. Learn to modify and adapt their techniques to meet the unique needs of their students
   3. Take courses that address multidimensional problems challenging *all* their students
   4. Understand the comprehensive support model (i.e., the relationship between the "self," family, school, community, and government)
   5. Learn from their students' families and communities
   6. Develop new ways to solve problems

7. Join community groups to solve societal problems
8. Join professional organizations
9. Attend professional conferences and inservice trainings

I am more convinced than before that new classroom structures ought to be formed to address the needs of *all* students. One thing is clear: When students are unhappy with the goings-on in the classroom, they respond by engaging in disruptive behaviors. Glasser (1986) explained that

> a disruptive student is no different from that same proverbial horse who would likely kick up his heels if he is held too long at the water when he isn't thirsty. Discipline is only a problem when students are forced into classes where they do not experience satisfaction. There are no discipline problems in any class where the students believe that if they make an effort to learn, they will gain some immediate satisfaction. To focus on discipline is to ignore the real problem: We will never be able to get students (or anyone else) to be in good order if, day after day, we try to force them to do what they do not find satisfying. If we insist on maintaining our traditional classroom structure, we will not be able to create classes that are significantly more satisfying than what we have now. (p. 12)

When a problem occurs in any learning situation, it indicates the teacher's inability to teach. There is a big difference between a teacher and an "imparter" of knowledge. When knowledge is imparted, it is easily regurgitated without critical thinking, but when knowledge is taught, it involves critical thinking, problem solving, application, analysis, synthesis, and evaluation. Consider the experiences of Dr. Kenneth Weaver, a former Peacecorper who went to teach the indigenes at Santa Catalina, Negros Oriental, Philippines on the South China Sea. In his essay "Experiences of a Peacecorper" (1994), he wrote,

In December 1973, with a new B.S. Degree in biology, I began a two-year service in rural public health in Santa Catalina, Negros Oriental, Philippines on the South China Sea. The conclusion of a conversation with myself in anticipation of the service's beginning was the observation that public health in the United States was probably without equal in the world. From this observation came a strategy for what was intended to increase my effectiveness— bring practices from home to the rural Philippines. For the first year, I lived according to this strategy. But public health is about bodily functions— waste disposal, reproduction, market sanitation, inoculation, and water purification. These personal topics are addressed when folks have a common frame of reference. How does one talk about waste disposal when there are no flush toilets? How can the potential sickness from the bacteria in a clear glass of water be explained to families who have used this water for generations? How can birth control be presented with no understanding of the cultural traditions of love, family, religion, or security? Thus, while the merits of my strategy to import home practices could be defended in theory, the result in practice was an "ugly American." Fortunately, the residents of Santa Catalina were a tolerant lot, but I suspect that quite a few folks were shaking their heads wondering who this strange American was and what he was doing here. An assessment of that first year produced only gloom. I was not happy; started projects were going nowhere; I had no friends, no buddies. Quitting was out of the question; besides, the oil embargo, political troubles, and employment prospects in the United States made returning home less palatable. Fortunately, the stream of consciousness that produced such a dismal evaluation flowed to a precious point of illumination. I was a visitor in this country. It was not for me to come and through word and practice tell my hosts what to do. Rather, here was a wonderful opportunity for me to learn, and I was certain that these folks had plenty to teach me. That slight rearrangement of perspective irrevocably changed my life. Literally, the next day people started to invite me into their homes, to join them in their activities, to share a meal, and play with their children. And through these experiences, they taught me and changed me until I was able to pass on what I knew in a way that was harmonious to that culture. The last month of my service I finally was able to teach (after 23 months of my stay). Folks began to ask how they could prevent catching a particular sickness, what they might do to ensure their baby's health, how they might have fewer children, what kinds of food they might eat, what would happen if the town's garbage was dumped into the ocean, how does a vaccine work. So, what's the implication for multicultural education? *Plenty!* Knowing another culture is being intellectually alive, looking at the same reality from different viewpoints, having a vantage point from which strengths and shortcomings of one's own culture can be appreciated, elevating quality of life, enriching interactions with others, reveling in our commonalities, pondering our differences, and thinking of ideas never before considered. My experiences at Santa Catalina will remain with me forever. (pp. 1-2)

Although Weaver's experiences were uniquely tied to cultural and global awareness, they demonstrate typical trials and tribulations of a teacher. Until teachers view themselves as persons whose job is to foster a healthy learning environment, students will not feel safe, and when students do not feel safe, they resist learning.

Many teachers tend to be "eclectic" in their teaching technique. However, this can be a cop-out explanation for a lack of strength in theoretical and practical orientations. I believe "good" teachers must be knowledgeable in different theoretical conceptualizations and models. Flimsy "eclecticism" is not the answer—thorough, in-depth knowledge is the key! Teachers cannot continue to be slaves to theories and models of teaching. For successful teaching to take place, each theory or model should respond to the unique need of each individual student. I strongly believe that *the best teaching strategy is the strategy that works for a particular student at a particular time in a particular place by a particular teacher or service provider.*

Surprisingly, teachers are hired and fired because of their theoretical orientations. How, then, can teachers teach individual differences and diversity among students when they fail to accept divergent viewpoints by diverse people? Theories reflect conceptualizations and models, which in turn foreshadow interventions and pedagogy. Let's look at the following theoretical models:

1. Psychodynamic Model—This model evolved from the intrapsychic phenomenon espoused by Sigmund Freud. It is a connection of theoretical constructs that denotes an eclectic use of ideas and activities (e.g., the use of play, drama, and art therapy to reduce inappropriate behaviors and enhance diversity).

2. Biophysical Model—This model emphasizes the organic origins of human behaviors (e.g., the use of medical or biochemical techniques to remediate classroom behaviors).

3. Environmental Model—This model connects the dominant theme in contemporary studies of human behaviors. Here, we find the sociological model (the way the society sees the individual) and ecological model (the way the individual interacts with the society; e.g., the knowledge of environmental and home problems that impinge upon learning).

4. Humanistic Model—This model is very student centered. There is no structure and no judgment, and the focus is on sensitivity or empathy (e.g., incorporating sensitivity and active listening can enhance students' and parents' participation).

5. Behavioral Model—This model deals with behavior changes that are observable and measurable (e.g., the use of behavior modification techniques can be reinforcing to students).

6. Cognitive Learning Model—This model assumes that an individual's perception of environmental stimuli affects

behavior changes. It is integrative in nature because humanism and behaviorism interface and interplay (e.g., the use of self-responsibility and Glasser's Reality Therapy can be effective in behavior management of students).

Based on these theoretical models, intervention or teaching strategies can be adequately organized. These models reflect divergent theoretical orientations that various professionals should use in working with students. For instance, when a teacher is a trained behaviorist, he or she cannot afford to downplay other strategies. Teachers should use other strategies to address the needs of all students when problem situations arise. Because it is common knowledge that students' behaviors are complex, what sense does it make to use a simple approach to ameliorate a complex multidimensional problem?

Many "good" teachers assume that "things have to be difficult or complex to be worthy." Algozzine (1993) proved this assumption wrong in his book *50 Simple Ways to Make Teaching More Fun.* He argued that many teaching situations in today's classrooms could be handled differently. For successful teaching, the axiom should be "no one method of teaching answers all our questions all the time." I was a member of a search committee to fill a teaching position. It was my duty to take the top applicant to lunch. In my discussion with this candidate, she indicated that she was a strict behaviorist, because her major professors in college were behaviorists. I still remember vividly the content of our conversation. I asked, "I appreciate your being a strict behaviorist. How can you teach a student who is still depressed because her cat died yesterday?" She responded, "What has the death of a cat got to do with classroom instruction?" I rephrased my question: "Let's assume that your student lost her grandmother who she loved so much. How would you handle it in your classroom assuming you had a test for all students?" She replied, "This student has to be ready for the test. What has the death of the grandmother got to do with the test that I have planned to conduct?" There was nothing wrong with this applicant's theoretical orientation; however, what was wrong was her failure to understand behaviorism and what it entails to enhance effective teaching and intervention practices. According to Gay (1992), effective teaching practices include doing the following:

1. Using cooperative group, team, and pair arrangements for learning as the normative structure instead of as the occasional exception

2. Using learning stations, multimedia, and interactive video to present information instead of some form of lecturing

3. Varying the format of learning activities frequently to incorporate more affective responses, motion, and movement

4. Establishing friendships between students and teachers

5. Creating genuine partnerships with students so that they are active participants in making decisions about how their learning experiences will occur and be evaluated

6. Changing rules and procedures that govern life in the classroom so they reflect some of the codes of behavior and participation styles of culturally different students

7. Devising ways for students to monitor and manage their own and each other's classroom behaviors

8. Developing an esprit de corps of "family" to give cohesion and focusing meaning to interpersonal relationships in the classroom

9. Including more human-centered and culturally different images, artifacts, experiences, and incidents in classroom decorations and as props for teaching. (p. 53)

Based on the aforementioned details, "good" teaching and intervention entails meeting the unique needs of each individual. Central to this idea are the pertinent questions that follow. Why, then, do "good" teachers in "good" schools fail to address the concepts of intraindividual and interindividual differences as they affect "good" teaching? Should "good" schools not be where real pedagogical power (i.e., the courage to reach every student) exists? Have teachers (even the "good" ones) ignored the best calling of their profession (i.e., to maximize the fullest potential of their students)? Should "good" teachers not have a broader frame of pedagogical reference? Johnson (1981) and Orlich, Harder, Callahan, and Gibson (2001) agreed that "good" teaching must incorporate the following:

1. The school milieu (i.e., the school culture)
2. A holistic view of instruction, especially for teaching perspectives and instruction decisions
3. Equity as the big picture
4. Goals, standards, and outcomes for instruction
5. Instruction design
6. Sequencing and organizing of instruction
7. Managing of the classroom environment
8. The process of questioning
9. Small-group discussions and cooperative learning
10. Inquiry teaching and higher-level thinking
11. Monitoring of student successes

These components of effective teaching cannot be ignored. In combination they make up different theoretical models (Obiakor, 1994; Obiakor & Algozzine, 1995). It is important that "good" teachers magnify their classroom energies by infusing divergent teaching models that include these:

1. Stimulus variability
2. Greater verve and rhythm
3. Verbal interactions
4. Divergent thinking
5. Use of dialect
6. Use of real-world experiences

7. A focus on people strengths
8. Cooperative learning
9. Peer/cross-age grouping
10. Peer tutoring and involvement
11. Parental empowerment
12. Instructional adaptability and modification
13. Individualized instruction
14. Community involvement
15. Cultural and linguistic valuing
16. Racial inclusion
17. Nonprejudicial assessment
18. Realistic expectations
19. Technological infusion
20. Global awareness

Also important is the appreciation of students' cultural backgrounds in the teaching-learning process. Bessent-Byrd (1995) identified some specific intervention techniques, including these:

1. Mnemonic activities
    a. *Audible recall:* repeats information orally to facilitate recall.
    b. *Iconic learning activities:* using pictures and figures of important data as memory aids.
    c. *Mediated learning:* matching associated images to information to provoke recall.
    d. *Acronym or acrostic stimulated recall:* first letter cueing to recall a series of terms.
2. Interactive activities
    a. *Keyboarding:* using a typewriter, word processor, or computer.
    b. *Enactive learning:* using manipulatives to aid learning.

c. *Group learning:* completing joint assignments working with others, peer tutoring.
3. Movement-for-learning activities
   a. *Theatrics:* role playing, pantomime, theater rehearsal techniques.
   b. *Rhythmics:* beating, clapping, or stepping to a pattern with recitation.
   c. *Locomotion:* marching, dancing during instruction or recitation.
   d. *Creative content construction:* writing content in poetry, creating and singing songs as a report, making up and erforming report as a lesson. (p. 143)

From my perspectives as a former high school teacher and an experienced college professor, I found that the following teaching techniques have worked for me.

1. Explaining fully what was expected of my students
2. Giving praise freely to students when it was earned
3. Presenting students with correct answers or methods first
4. Teaching students by example
5. Disciplining students without humiliating them
6. Providing students with constructive activities to replace activities I wanted to inhibit
7. Using concrete objects for demonstrations to my students
8. Progressing to more difficult tasks when simpler tasks were mastered by students
9. Creating students' interests and attention
10. Spelling for students any words that are difficult to understand because of my accent
11. Structuring my students' classroom environment
12. Giving students choices whenever possible and following through
13. Encouraging students' attempts to perform a task

14. Smiling a lot and reminding my students about the beauties of the teaching profession and life

15. Using personal experiences in teaching to stimulate students' critical thinking and problem-solving skills

16. Using *ladies and gentlemen* to refer to my students

17. Focusing on outcomes or what students have learned and not on tests

18. Helping my students continuously search for "new" meaning as we explore "new" learning

19. Providing universal themes while responding to my students' unique needs

20. Evaluating my students' growth in more ways than one (see Obiakor, 1994, p. 85)

The teaching and intervention techniques addressed repeatedly in this chapter have been proven by research and practice. However, I do not believe we should impose them on teachers; instead, the idea is to make sure that teachers and schools (especially those "good" ones) shift their paradigms in the teaching-learning process. When instructions are based on *one* theoretical model, a particular frame of pedagogical reference becomes dominant. Many supposedly "good" schools are philosophically narrow—they take fewer risks in building a system of instructional programming that fits students' realities. As a result, the end justifies the means! The critical question then is this: Should "good" schools not be where "good" teaching prevails? Consider the following pertinent cases.

Case 23

Darrell was an African American student who attended a well-known "good" school. He excelled in all classroom activities. His teacher asked him and his class to choose world leaders who have made historical differences in their respective countries. After choosing their preferences, students were required to research and present their findings to their classmates. Students were asked questions in the end, and they acted and responded like these leaders as they were being videotaped. Darrell focused his research on Malcolm X, while his Anglo American classmates focused on Anglo American leaders in Europe and the United States. Before the videotaping began, the teacher called Darrell, noting, "I do not think you should do your work on Malcolm X. He was a radical. You should do your work on Martin Luther King, Jr." Darrell felt devastated and told his mother. When she spoke to the teacher, he responded, "If he does not do the assignment on Martin Luther King, Jr., he will not receive full points. I don't know why you Blacks like Malcolm X." Because Darrell had spent so much time and energy doing his research on Malcolm X, he presented his findings, and his classmates liked the presentation. As the teacher promised, he did not give Darrell full points because he did his research on Malcolm X. Darrell's mother was upset. She reported the case to the principal, who later supported the teacher.

Traditional Problems and Solutions

In Case 23, there are apparent problems that include the following:

1. Darrell's teacher demonstrated his personal dislike for Malcolm X.
2. Darrell's leadership preference was downplayed because he chose Malcolm X.
3. Darrell's teacher played the classical race card of Whites choosing who should be a Black leader (i.e., classic racial domination).
4. Darrell and his mother were not allowed to assert their positions.
5. Darrell's classroom activities turned out to be prejudicial.
6. Darrell's ethnic pride was demeaned.

7. The principal blindly supported Darrell's prejudicial evaluation by the teacher.

Traditionally, many CLD students are not allowed to maximize their learning potential by unprepared teachers. Here was a teacher who gave his students the opportunity to research and present their ideas! This assignment could have had serious multicultural implications. However, the teacher failed to see the opportunity to infuse antibias learning and inclusive classroom activities. In other words, the stage that was set for global awareness resulted in cultural and racial devaluing. When such devaluing is picked up by students and their parents, harmonious relationships between school and family or school and community are destroyed.

Culturally Responsive Solutions

Case 23 presents the case of a teacher's inflexibility on cultural valuing. This teacher failed to follow through on the creative opportunities that he provided for his students. Ironically, the school principal blindly supported his teacher without going into the mind's eyes of the parent. These problems have several pedagogical implications. Based on Case 23, I believe a truly "good" teacher should do the following:

1. Be globally and culturally aware
2. Promote equitable teacher-student relationships
3. Display flexibility in the context of a structured learning environment
4. Value a parent's opinion in the teaching-learning process
5. Possess a repertoire of varied teaching styles and adjust them to accommodate varied learning styles
6. Shift his or her paradigm
7. Get out of his or her comfort zone
8. Provide opportunities for growth at all times
9. Care for his or her students

10. Understand the basic ingredients of good teaching (e.g., accurate assessment of student performance)

Key Points

Based on the aforementioned details, here are some important key points:

1. Teaching involves self-awareness and self-responsibility.
2. Teaching, when done right, allows students to assert their opinions.
3. Teaching involves the uplifting of human potential.
4. Teaching, when inappropriately done, demeans students' energies and strengths.
5. Teaching is enhanced when the learning environment is appropriately manipulated.

Case 24

Pete was a brilliant Hispanic American student who attended a "good" school in a heterogeneous community. This school was noted for its reputable "good" teachers; however, there were a series of complaints from minority students and their parents about these teachers. In Pete's class, his teacher ignored him when he raised his hand to respond to classroom discussions. When he was called upon, his answers were not given serious attention. Surprisingly, when Anglo American students gave similar answers, they were prompted and given praises. Pete told his father, who came to talk with the teacher. This teacher responded, "This is my class. I do whatever I want to do. You do not tell me how to do my job." The teacher continued with this behavior, and Pete began to have school problems. For instance, he began to be tardy and absent in school and began to hate school.

Traditional Problems and Solutions

In Case 24, there are apparent problems that include the following:

1. Pete attended a supposed "good" school, but this school was defined from a very narrow perspective.
2. Minority students and their parents complained about the insensitivity of the teachers in the "good" school, and no one listened.
3. Pete's potential in class was not maximized.
4. Pete received no prompts, praises, or acknowledgments from his teacher.
5. Pete's teacher failed to take advantage of collaborative and consultative energies between him and the parent.
6. Pete's learning environment was extremely restrictive.
7. Pete's teacher did not have the courage to teach.

Traditionally, supposedly "good" teachers appear invincible. These teachers frequently play God—they do not believe they can be corrected. The perceptual notion of "good" teachers and "good" schools seems to be overplayed by the media. Even though we know what is right, we frequently get bamboozled by phony meritocracy. Here was a teacher who cared less about his minority students and their parents, yet he was regarded as a "good" teacher. How can a school that cares less about some of its students and families be a "good" school? Pete's learning environment was clearly restrictive, and his self-concepts and intelligence were marginalized by the "good" school.

Culturally Responsive Solutions

Case 24 exposes typical insensitivity of some teachers in school programs. As it appears, Pete was treated as an "invisible" youth, but he refused to be invisible. The behavior of Pete's teacher is not uncommon in many of today's classrooms. Apparently, the more things change, the more they remain the same. Based on Case 24, I believe a truly "good" teacher should do the following:

1. Be culturally aware and sensitive
2. Know what it means to be a teacher
3. Respond to the unique needs of his or her students
4. Work collaboratively and consultatively with parents
5. Connect him- or herself to the community
6. Challenge his or her thinking
7. Be flexible in his or her teaching technique
8. Be a good professional
9. Be a problem solver and not a problem creator
10. Modify and adapt as needed

Key Points

Based on the aforementioned details, here are some important key points:

1. Teaching involves "quality with a heart."
2. Teaching involves leadership and problem solving.
3. Teaching, when done right, maximizes the fullest potential of students.
4. Teaching involves antibias thinking.
5. Teaching involves individualized instruction in a nonrestrictive environment.

Case 25

Chang was an Asian American student of Chinese origin. He attended a "good" neighborhood school. He was pretty good in mathematics and the sciences, and his dream was to become a medical doctor. He did his assignments and homework on time, yet his teachers (especially his mathematics teacher) were frequently displeased with him. On many occasions, he did the mathematics homework he was given with methods different from what the teacher had taught him. In fact, he did it with simpler, less complicated methods taught him by his parents, who also were great scientists. However, Chang's teacher consistently gave him a "B" grade because he did not use his methods. This became a major problem in the school. When Chang's parents challenged the teacher, he became defensive and told the parents, "This is my class. Your son is supposed to follow my method. Why do you Asians think that you are so smart?" In no time, Chang's teacher shared his experiences with other faculty members in the faculty lounge. Surprisingly, all his colleagues believed him, and none of them came to the rescue of Chang and his parents. Chang was frustrated and began to hate school. Seeing this devastating picture, Chang's parents transferred him to a new school.

Traditional Problems and Solutions

In Case 25, there are apparent problems that include the following:

1. Chang's teacher was simply not a "good" teacher.
2. Chang's learning environment became very restrictive for him.
3. In more ways than one, Chang's teacher succeeded in getting rid of Chang from his class.
4. Chang's teacher failed to be flexible in his teaching techniques.
5. Chang's teacher failed to adapt or modify instruction for him.
6. Chang's teacher failed to be confidential in the faculty lounge.
7. The colleagues of Chang's teacher believed him without challenging his narrow pedagogical frame of reference.

Traditionally, many teachers fail to see the parent as a team player. In Case 25, the wonderful support of Chang's parents was misconstrued. A "good" teacher would have taken advantage of the parents' support. Instead, this support became a problem that had far-reaching effects on Chang. His learning environment became so traumatic and restrictive that his parents had to transfer him to a new school. What an unnecessary disruption in Chang's school life!

Culturally Responsive Solutions

Case 25 reiterates typical scenarios for many students. When parents are not involved in their children's education, teachers complain, and when they are too involved, teachers complain. What do teachers really want from parents? Do they not want them to be empowered in the educational developments of their children? Very often, children like Chang suffer when parents and teachers fail to get along. Based on Case 25, I believe a truly "good" teacher should do the following:

1. Meet the unique needs of his or her students
2. Not be at war with parents
3. Respond to intraindividual and interindividual differences in his or her students
4. Work collaboratively and consultatively with parents and guardians
5. Maintain confidentiality on students' information
6. Value his or her professional integrity
7. Make the student's learning environment conducive to the student's needs
8. Maximize the learning potential of his or her students
9. Have real pedagogical power
10. Have "soul"

Key Points

Based on the aforementioned details, here are some important key points:

1. Teaching involves flexibility in instructional delivery.
2. Teaching involves the "heart and soul."
3. Teaching, when done inappropriately, can be an unworthy profession.
4. Teaching involves equal partnership with parents.
5. Teaching involves helping every student maximize his or her fullest potential.

Case 26

Drennon was a brilliant Native American student who attended a "good" school. His dream was to be a lawyer. His parents were card-carrying Native Americans who frequently dressed in traditional attire and participated in native rituals. Drennon's teacher gave group work in reading and other assignments. Unfortunately, Drennon's classmates consistently refused to work with him. On one occasion, his teacher gave the class a reading assignment. He wanted to read with a partner, but his classmates told him that they already had partners. Sadly, the only person who read alone was Drennon, and this never seemed to bother his classmates and teacher. Drennon's parents brought this issue to the attention of the principal, who promised to do something about it but never did anything. As a result, Drennon was moved to a new school to avoid further psychological problems.

Traditional Problems and Solutions

In Case 26, there are apparent problems that include the following:

1. Drennon's potential to succeed was not maximized in the class.
2. Drennon endured psychological and self-concept problems.
3. Drennon's classmates refused to work with him.
4. Drennon's teacher encouraged phony collaborative learning typical in many classrooms and educational programs.
5. Underlying racial assumptions were playing themselves out in this class.
6. The teacher's lack of cultural competence was very visible.
7. Drennon was moved to a new school to avoid further psychological problems.

Traditionally, schools talk about how to enhance cooperative learning through peer relations. How can cooperative learning function where classmates refuse to work with classmates or where teachers do not encourage it? It appears that in many "good" schools, the issue of minority student exclusion does not matter. Such exclusive practices to a large measure demonstrate the unpreparedness of teachers to (a) value individual differences (e.g., culture, race, and socioeconomic status); (b) tackle societal problems and community responsibilities (e.g., racism, xenophobia, and unfairness); (c) learn from real experiences of minorities (e.g., students, parents, educators, and leaders); (d) incorporate innovative thinking (e.g., emotional intelligence, critical thinking, and creativity) as they teach *all* students; and (e) infuse multicultural models and cases (e.g., daily happenings in the society).

Culturally Responsive Solutions

Case 26 reveals the traditional problem of "saying one thing and doing another thing." Many "good" schools indicate that they are culturally sensitive and socioeconomically receptive to students. What do we expect? Teachers are poorly prepared, ill-prepared, or unprepared to deal with these issues. Culture and socioeconomics are viewed as deficits— the focus is frequently on building the 3 Rs (reading, writing, and arithmetic) and improving norm-referenced standardized scores. These narrow foci make preparing students for life's realities very difficult. Based on Case 26, I believe a truly "good" teacher should so the following:

1. Educate him- or herself about things he or she does not know
2. Avoid assumptions about race, culture, and socioeconomic status
3. Integrate a wide variety of cultures into his or her teaching
4. Be knowledgeable and creative
5. Value and celebrate differences that students bring to class
6. Integrate individuals in projects and assignments
7. Create bridges that connect people
8. Create an atmosphere that empowers students
9. Encourage students to maximize their potential
10. View the classroom as a machine that, when fine-tuned, can do wonderful things

Key Points

Based on the aforementioned details, here are some important key points:

1. Teaching, when inappropriately done, disempowers students.
2. Teaching can build communities.
3. Teaching should respond to shifts in demography.
4. Teaching involves sensitivity and flexibility.
5. Teaching involves cultural understanding.

Strategic Lessons Learned

This chapter has focused on teaching and intervention in schools. Although it is common knowledge that identification, referral, labeling, categorization, placement, and inclusion are all basic ingredients of teaching, "good" teachers have pedagogical power to put these ingredients in proper perspective. Truly "good" teachers can help make schools "good"—they can also make sure that their "good" schools respond to demographic shifts in paradigms. My premise is that "good" schools ought to be where teachers have the courage to teach. In addition, "good" schools should be where teachers modify and adapt instructional techniques to reach *all* students. What follows are important principles for "good" teachers:

1. "Good" teaching is the engine behind "good" schools.
2. Teachers must incorporate their students' experiences into their classrooms.
3. Teaching cannot be divorced from identification, referral, labels, categories, and placement.
4. "Good" teachers manage student stressors.
5. Fraudulent teaching practices result from poor preparation.
6. Differences do not mean deficits in classroom interaction.
7. Learning environments must be manipulated to meet the unique needs of *all* students.
8. Families are equal partners in the teaching-learning process.
9. Principals are accountable for what goes on in their schools.
10. "Good" principals should be analytical of what teachers tell them.
11. The faculty lounge should not be where teachers conspire to get rid of students.
12. Divergent teaching techniques are necessary for students.

13. Teacher expectations can help or hurt students.
14. Teacher-student and student-student interactions are necessary to enhance classroom harmony.
15. Classroom instructions must respond to intraindividual and interindividual differences in students, teachers, and parents.

7

❦———❦

The Dream School:
The Good School

Throughout this book, I have discussed the "good" school phenomenon and challenged our definition of good schools using pertinent cases. I believe we must redefine "good" schools to tackle society's realities. I vehemently argue that good schools cannot be defined from the perspectives of race, color, language, socioeconomics, and national origin. Unfortunately, "good" schools have been defined puritanically. Schools in "rich" neighborhoods and schools located in homogeneous communities have been viewed as "good" schools. My premise is that a truly "good" school must be culturally, racially, linguistically, and socioeconomically heterogeneous. Such a school must reflect demographic shifts in paradigms and powers. Additionally, in such a school, students will not be misidentified, misassessed, mislabeled, miscategorized, misplaced, and misinstructed (Obiakor, 2000b).

In this chapter, I focus on my dream school, the "good school" where *all* students' potential will be maximized to the fullest. My dream school will be neither (a) a *White* school nor a *Black* school, (b) a *Latino* school nor an *Asian American* school, (c) a *Native American* school nor a *special* school, (d) a *rich* school nor a *poor* school, (e) a school for *smart people* nor a school for the *not-so-smart* people. My dream school will be a "good" school where all the above flourish, that is, a school where opportunities and choices for growth are created by well-prepared teachers who understand the true meaning of the teaching profession. Simply put, in my dream school, teachers will be truly "good" teachers who have the courage to teach with their real pedagogical power (Dewey, 1958; Henderson & Bibens, 1970; Hilliard, 1992, 1995; Johnson, 1981; Kohl, 1988; Ladson-Billings, 1994; Orlich et al., 2001; Palmer, 1998). In my dream school, "culture" will be a non-controversial phenomenon that increases the "goodness" and *quality* of school and classroom activities. In fact, my dream school, the good school, will:

1. Be located in all neighborhoods (i.e., suburban, urban, rural, and inner-city areas)

2. Have minority and majority students to reflect demographic shifts

3. Have minority and majority teachers to reflect demographic shifts

4. Have culturally competent teachers

5. Produce culturally competent students

6. Be dedicated to excellence

7. Believe in "quality with a heart"

8. Have teachers with "soul"

9. Respond to student stressors and individual differences

10. Address issues of student learning styles and multiple intelligences

11. Encourage all students to maximize their potential

12. Empower parents and community members in all their activities

13. Work collaboratively, consultatively, and cooperatively with parents despite their cultural, racial, and socio-economic backgrounds
14. Not get rid of students indiscriminately
15. Try its best to educate *all* students
16. Prepare students to be responsible and productive citizens through self-knowledge, self-esteem, and self-empowerment
17. Prepare students to be nationally and globally aware
18. Go beyond traditions to be creative
19. Be abreast of the times in how it hires its administrators
20. Have administrators who care for students
21. Make multiple voices heard in classroom activities
22. Not support making some students "invisible"
23. Create and maintain learning communities
24. Not be puritanical (i.e., not have a perfectionist mentality)
25. Have truly "good" teachers who will teach *reality*

Based on the aforementioned details, it seems clear to me that my dream school, the "good" school, will have four basic operational dimensions:

1. It will function with a comprehensive support model (CSM).
2. It will become a learning community.
3. It will become a place to master the craft of teaching.
4. It will foster a multidimensional teaching-learning process.

Functioning With the Comprehensive Support Model

Everyone wants a dream school that can meet the needs of *all* students! My dream school will be a truly "good" school

where best practices are manifested in all educational programming for *all* students. In such a "good" school, the CSM
must flourish. Based on the CSM, the "self," family, school,
community, and government will be collaboratively and
consultatively involved. The "self" will be involved because
without the personal powers of all entities involved in learning, self-responsibility may not be maximized. The family
will be important because it is the cornerstone of the student
and the bridge that connects the student with the school. The
school will be a part of the CSM because it will have teachers
and professionals who have the power to shift their paradigms regarding demographic changes. The community will
be an important part of the CSM because it will provide a
variety of opportunities and choices for children and youth,
parents, schools, and governmental entities to come together.
To make the CSM work, the government will not divorce itself
from the happenings in families, schools, and communities.
Governmental entities will be involved in generating equitable policies that elicit the multiple voices of its citizenry.

In my dream school, *all* components of the CSM will listen
to each other and communicate as they empower each other.
The blame game will be over as diverse positive forces collaborate, consult, and cooperate for the common good. In my
dream school, the whole village will be at work, because "it
takes a *responsible* village to raise a *responsible* child" (see
Obiakor, 1994). The Milwaukee Catalyst (1998) reiterated
these ideas to press for effective educational reforms based on
research. This organization highlighted five essential supports for school learning that must be in place to improve
school-community relationships:

1. Effective school leadership
2. Family-community partnerships
3. A school environment that supports learning
4. Effective staff development and collaboration
5. A quality instructional program (p. 1)

As the Milwaukee Catalyst (1998) concluded,

Making practices like these a reality requires major changes—not only in the classroom but also in the way the entire school is run and in its ties with students, families, and the community. Making these changes allows the schools to focus their resources and attention on improving teaching, learning, and student achievement for all children. (p. 2)

In my dream school, community forces will be an integral part of its daily functioning. We will not ignore any part of the whole village!

Becoming a Learning Community

In my dream school, the focus will be on maintaining a learning community. According to Peterson (1992),

Community in itself is more important to learning than any method or technique. When community exists, learning is strengthened—everyone is smarter, more ambitious, and productive. Well-formed ideas and intentions amount to little without a community to bring them to life. (p. 2)

He added,

Life in a learning community is helped along by the interests, ideas, and support of others. Social life is not snuffed out; it is nurtured and used to advance learning in the best way possible. Learning is social. . . . The position taken is that learning awakens a variety of internal processes that operate only when the child is interacting with others in his [her] environment and in cooperation with his [her] peers. Even mainstream educators are beginning to recognize that education fails when it focuses solely on the accumulation of demonstrable facts and skill. An image is taking shape that acknowledges a more complex and irreducible phenomenon, the social person. (p. 3)

My dream school will be a learning community where learning is shared with a *heart*. In such a learning community, life in the classroom will be less intense, and there will be fewer restrictions like the ones that were shown in the cases discussed throughout this book. A well-organized learning community leads to holistic teaching. As Peterson (1992) concluded, holistic teaching entails the following:

1. *Teacher orientation* to help students grow in complicated and critical ways
2. *A view of knowledge* to help people construct meaning through experiences
3. *Meaning-centered teaching* to help knowledge to be personalized as people search for meaning
4. *Skills* to help to negotiate, express, and develop knowledge
5. *Curriculum* to help connect students' lives to learning
6. *Connectedness* to help students build upon what makes sense to them
7. *Collaboration* to help students and teachers learn together
8. *Accountability* to help students to be accountable for their own learning and teachers to be accountable for what they do in the classroom
9. *Students* who participate in planning and evaluating their education
10. *Competence* to demonstrate how people express meaning, solve problems, work with others, and critique intelligently

Becoming a Place to Master the Craft of Teaching

"Good" teachers are "good" students. In my dream school, the "good school," teachers will know what it means to be a teacher, and they will value their profession as change agents. Many years ago, Dewey (1960) wrote,

Constant and uniform relations in change and a knowledge of them in "laws," are not a hindrance to freedom, but a necessary factor in coming to be effectively that which we have the capacity to grow into. Social conditions interact with the preferences of an individual (that are his or her individuality) in a way favorable to actualizing freedom only when they develop intelligence, not abstract knowledge and abstract thought, but power of vision and reflection. For these take effect in making preference, desire, and purpose more flexible, alert, and resolute. Freedom has too long been thought of as indeterminate power operating in a closed and ended world. In its reality, freedom is a resolute will operating in a world in some respects indeterminate, because open and moving toward a new future. (p. 287)

Based on Dewey's statement, in my "good" school, human beings will search for answers to problems (Toffler, 1982). In other words, "good" teachers will be liberated when they master their craft through preservice and inservice trainings. Because my dream school will be made up of diverse students and teachers, individuals who refuse to leave their comfort zones or shift their paradigms will be unhappy campers. Simply put, in my good school, learning will be a continuous process of development! Guillaume, Zuniga-Hill, and Yee (1995) postulated that teachers of diverse students should do the following:

1. Develop a knowledge base about diverse ethnic groups and have multiple opportunities to examine personal attitudes toward students of color

2. Develop culturally and linguistically supportive strategies and approaches that make learning available and equitable for all students

   3. Have ample exposure to students of diverse
      backgrounds and to teachers who can model
      appropriate instructional approaches
   4. Commit to professional growth regarding is-
      sues of diversity (p. 70)

   I believe that to understand teaching is to understand communication. In my dream school, teachers, principals, and
school district personnel will learn to communicate with others. Teachers who are good imparters of knowledge may not
necessarily be good communicators. Effective communication will create workplace success and mutual awareness
(Harris-Obiakor, 2000). In my dream school, teachers will
answer the following questions:

   1. Why is effective communication so necessary?
   2. What is communication all about?
   3. What are the barriers that affect the communication
      process?
   4. What are the tips for being a good communicator?

"Good" teachers must be good communicators. How many of
us have ever wondered why students do not follow instructions? Maybe students do not understand teachers' directions.
As a consequence, in my dream school, teachers will:

   1. Understand that communication is a two-way process
      between the sender and the receiver
   2. Be sensitive and aware
   3. Take great interest in others
   4. Be specific
   5. Keep messages clear in terms that will be understood
   6. Accept the fact that people do things for their own per-
      sonal reasons
   7. Adjust messages to meet circumstances
   8. Be sincere

9. Know what they do not know

10. Not be who they are not

I am convinced that there are tremendous requirements and demands of being an educator (see Hoyle, 1975; Obiakor et al., 1998). Hoyle (1975) described these demands in the following quote:

The teacher has a much wider public than his/her pupils and colleagues. Outside the school a number of groups have their own expectations of the teacher's role. These groups include the parents of pupils, local counselors and others who have responsibilities for education, the members of various voluntary organizations which take an interest in education, and members of Parent-Teacher Associations. In addition, members of the public have their conceptions of the teacher. The degree to which these expectations directly impinge upon the teacher and shape his [her] conception of his [her] role varies from society to society. (p. 69)

These demands require that "good" teachers develop techniques to survive in today's changing world. In my dream school, teachers will possess "business beatitudes" (Beattie, 1982) that include character, enthusiasm, courage, responsibility, persistence, endurance, self-control, integrity, confidence, knowledge, determination, ambition, teamwork, and wisdom. In such a school, teachers will be frantically working to (a) build the knowledge base, (b) examine the classroom culture, (c) plan and deliver instruction, (d) negotiate the roles of teaching, (e) build self-concepts through self-efficacy, (f) restructure learning environments, (g) enhance learning with technologies and resources, and (h) work beyond the classroom (see Obiakor et al., 1998). Mastering the craft of teaching is to be aware of positive changes that lead to the "common good." Surely, "good" teachers in my dream school will be ready to meet the challenges of the new century. They will expand their learning opportunities, value diversity,

consult with families and community members, and provide needed support for collaborative systems:

As it appears, educators cannot afford to be divorced
from their communities, and their communities cannot
afford to be divorced from them. In sum, challenges that
face communities will continue to be visible in schools,
and the ways educators deal with these challenges will
be particularly important in the years ahead. (Obiakor
et al., 1998, p. 152)

Fostering a Multidimensional
Teaching-Learning Process

As individuals are different, so must the teaching-learning
process be. Ironically, this idea has not taken precedence in
today's classrooms and schools. Our research and practice on
effective schools and effective teaching have been somewhat
confusing (Bliss, Firestone, & Richards, 1991). For instance,
we talk about responding to individual differences as we
teach, but very often differences are viewed as deficits. In my
dream school, we will not only talk about differences, we will
use them to strengthen and beautify our classrooms. My experiences tell me that people consistently shift their paradigms
to respond to society's changes. Additionally, my experiences
tell me that those who refuse to shift their paradigms affect
others with their retrogressive behaviors—most frequently,
people's futures are negatively affected. For an example,
consider Case 27.

Case 27

Just a few years ago, on October 6, 1995, I was on one of
my trips to present a paper at the Council for Children With
Behavior Disorders International Convention in Dallas,
Texas. Because I detest driving, I took a Greyhound bus

from Emporia, Kansas, to Wichita, Kansas, where my flight was scheduled to take off at around 6 a.m. My bus left Emporia around 2:30 a.m. en route to Wichita. Around 3 a.m., the bus driver stopped in El Dorado for some rest time. I went briefly to use the restroom, and by the time I came out, the bus had left me in El Dorado. I was stranded and frustrated in the strange hours of the morning. My frustration rose because I did not want to miss my flight in Wichita. I began to talk to anyone who would listen at this rest area. I knew the dangers involved, but I had to take the risk. I asked the people (I mean people of all races and cultures) that I saw for a ride to Wichita. Even the African Americans I asked did not respond—they ignored me. I lost hope until I asked a White man (Mr. C. W. Sisemore), who surprised me—he agreed. Remember, it was around 3:40 a.m. in the morning! This White man looked like a construction worker—he wore some mud-ridden "cowboy" clothes. I was dumbfounded that he consented to give me (a Black man) a ride this early in the morning. I thought that the well-dressed people, especially the African Americans, would consent to give me a ride, but I was wrong. Anyway, my newfound friend began to speed to catch the bus. We did not catch the bus, but we got there not long after the bus arrived in Wichita. Luckily, my luggage was still on the bus. Mr. C. W. Sisemore waited for me to get my luggage, and he gave me a ride to the Wichita airport, where I took my flight to Dallas. I tried to give him some money to repay his kindness, but he refused.

Although this case may appear a bit far-fetched, many of today's teachers can learn from Mr. Sisemore. Even though I took a risk to ask for a ride in the early hours of the morning, he took a greater risk to give me a ride. Not only do such risks reduce stereotypes and generalizations, they also make long-term positive impressions on people. How many of us would demonstrate such courage when people are down? Who would have imagined in these days of racial mistrust that a White man would give a ride to a Black man in the early hours of the morning? I am reminded of the biblical parable of the "Good Samaritan," in which the supposedly "good" people left a man stranded and the unrespected stranger saved him. As it appears, Mr. Sisemore had nothing to gain by giving me a ride, yet he took his time and risk to give me a ride. Teachers can learn a lot from him! In my dream school, teachers will take risks like Mr. Sisemore and be rewarded for taking them.

Consider another example in Case 28, the case of the "Danshiki Man," who frequently wore his African attire to portray his pride as a Black man of African descent.

Case 28

The "Danshiki Man" was an African American who directed a Black program at a major university. He was known for his pride about Africa. In fact, he was the faculty sponsor for the Black Students' Union and the Organization of African Students. For instance, he invited Africans to support his programs and wore African attire to school. As a result, the university administration never wanted to mess with him—they were scared that this man who knew so much about Africa would take them to task. Nobody tried to bother him! He was virtually free to do whatever he wanted to do. The Danshiki Man had two daughters who were also students at the same university. These daughters were "beautiful, black, and brilliant" and commanded great respect on campus. Before long, one handsome Nigerian who was pursuing a graduate degree in chemical engineering became captivated by one of the Danshiki Man's daughters. He came from a rich royal family. He made a pass at the daughter, and she accepted. The two of them began to date, and she started strategizing on how to introduce him to her family. The Danshiki Man heard through the grapevine that his daughter was dating a Nigerian. He confronted the daughter with the news, and she honestly acknowledged that she was falling in love with this Nigerian. The Danshiki Man was angry and asked the daughter, "Why are you dating an African? Could you not see other African American men? Do you really know what you're doing? How will your kids look? Do you plan to live with him in the jungle? What will people say when they hear that my daughter is married to an African?" The daughter responded, "I thought you loved Africans, Daddy. I can't believe you are bigoted and closed-minded toward them." The Danshiki Man repeated, "I don't care what you say. Do not marry an African! Africans are backward." Out of respect for the Danshiki Man, the daughter stopped dating the Nigerian, and their wonderful relationship ended. They were both emotionally devastated.

Again, this case might be far-fetched, but it depicts the fact that people of similar race can be closed-minded. Even though the Danshiki Man wore African attire to show his pride for Africa, he was phony. He preached what he never practiced. Some teachers play this kind of self-destructive game in schools today. They think that being multicultural means wearing cultural attire, eating at Taco Bell, or using chopsticks instead of a fork at Chinese restaurants. I am convinced that "good" teachers frequently go beyond tradition to challenge their thinking and action. "Goodness" must also go beyond race, culture, language, and socioeconomics. In my dream school, teachers like the Danshiki Man will be challenged, retrained, and retooled. Paley (2000) recounted her experiences in teaching a multicultural classroom. In doing this, she presented a model for self-examination of teacher prejudices. Such self-examination is necessary to help students reach for the top. In spite of the personal and emotional challenges posed by her students, Paley remained "capable of setting the limits and confronting children with misperceptions, misunderstandings, contradictions, and self-destructive behavior" (cited in Comer & Poussaint, 2000, p. x). As Paley pointed out,

the challenge in teaching is to find a way of communicating to each child the idea that his or her special quality is understood, is valued, and can be talked about. It is not

easy, because we are influenced by the fears and prejudices, apprehensions and expectations, which have become a carefully hidden part of every one of us. (p. xx)

In the teaching-learning process, my dream school's goal
will be multidimensional. Johnson (1981) agreed that multi-
dimensionality should be followed in responding to school
order, student interest, school spirit, student discipline, classroom instruction, classroom discussion and mastery, planning class period, study skills, homework, classroom organization, behavior management, selecting and organizing
intervals, organizing time, evaluating and testing students,
reporting to parents and students, and dealing with written
work of students. Even in designing new programs, multi-
dimensionality should be the key! For example, the School
District of Shorewood, Wisconsin (1997) offered multiple
programs to enrich the minds of its students. These programs
included school newspapers, accelerated reader programs,
battle of the books, junior great books, writers' club, literary
club, young authors' conference, geography hunt, science
fair, special projects, and a stock market game. This district
also offered a variety of educational activities to provide
opportunities and choices for its students. These activities
included accelerated courses (e.g., foreign language and or-
chestra), cocurricular activities (e.g., student council and play
production), challenge program activities (e.g., international
pen pals and quiz bowl), advanced classes (e.g., anthropol-
ogy and physics), and extracurriculars (e.g., jazz ensemble
and multicultural council). In my dream school, a variety of
enrichment programs will be provided to maximize the fullest potential of students and to expose them to life's realities.
Teachers who lead these activities will be rewarded through
merit pay and other forms of professionally enhancing
activities.

In my dream school, identification, referral, assessment,
and placement will be instructionally related. As a result, they
will be done nondiscriminatorily. What follows are important
things to consider in assessing students in my dream school:

1. Needs of the student across all components of the eco-logical system in which he or she lives
2. Instruction as the primary purpose of assessment
3. The importance of emphasizing functional levels rather than qualified statements of performance based on extrapolations from limited samples of behavior
4. The functioning of a child at home, on the bus, on the playground, and with peers as more relevant than his or her performance in a specialist's office (e.g., offices of counselors, diagnosticians, and school psychologists)
5. Where children are, what they can do, and what they are doing, not what they cannot do
6. The importance of using assessment to determine what the child needs to become the most competent human being possible
7. Intelligence as a phenomenon that can be defined in multiple ways

Grilliot (1995), Ladson-Billings (2000), Mickler (1994), and Ysseldyke et al. (2000) reiterated these considerations in their works. For instance, Mickler concluded,

Teachers can help all students learn their intellectual and academic abilities are far broader than those tested by traditional assessment techniques and those required to complete the kind of academic tasks that characterize unidimensional classrooms. Educators (and parents) must extensively explore their own personally held views about intelligence and learning and how those views critically influence their classroom decisions. (p. 149)

In my dream school, teachers will manage students' behaviors without bias or prejudice. They will make sure that they consider the student's *age, culture, circumstance,* and *situation* before they determine that his or her behavior departs from acceptable standards. They will make sure that they document the frequency and duration of behaviors even when such behaviors do depart from acceptable standards (see Obiakor & Algozzine, 1995). As a result, they will (a) plan activities that capture student attention, (b) model expected behaviors, (c) catch students being good, (d) give rewards and praises as needed, and (e) not label behaviors as "bad" because they depart from personal idiosyncrasies. In my dream school, teachers will do the following:

1. Try new experiences
2. Cope with change
3. Work cooperatively
4. Respect other cultures, races, and beliefs
5. See different points of view
6. Be open-minded
7. Solve problems
8. Demonstrate an inquiring attitude
9. Avoid name-calling and teasing
10. Participate in group action
11. Challenge stereotypes
12. Take actions against unfair situations or comments
13. Confront injustice
14. Practice inclusion
15. Recognize self in relation to the larger community

Hall (1999), Lovitt (2000), and Orlich et al. (2001) supported these principles for dealing with inappropriate behaviors. Hall suggested that creative resources be made necessary to enhance an antibias classroom "rooted in the singular belief that children will grow up to be flexible, accepting, open-minded, and nonjudgmental adults if they can live, learn, and play with the rich diversity of the human experience" (p. 2). On the other hand, Lovitt identified specific strategies to prevent school failure and dropout when he noted that

the physical environment of the classroom can affect students' motivation to learn just as the environment of a factory can affect workers' production. In most class-rooms, the teacher stands at the front of the room and students sit at desks arranged in rows and columns. Seating arrangements can have a great impact on students' motivation and their interactions in a class. A number of other factors that can affect student behaviors—and hence comfort and motivation—include room lighting, colors, type of furniture, number of people in the room, and room temperature. (p. 45)

In the same fashion, Orlich et al. (2001) advocated a social constructivist model that encompasses a range of beliefs and pedagogical approaches that center on maximizing the child's learning potential. According to Orlich et al., "effective teaching involves understanding students' existing cognitive structures and providing appropriate learning activities to assist them" (p. 53).

In my dream school, inclusion will be the modus operandi (i.e., inclusion will be put into proper practical perspectives). In other words, inclusive policies in the teaching-learning process will be the prevailing principle. Halvorsen and Neary (2001) confirmed that inclusive programming is necessary, especially in service delivery, planning and curriculum development, best practices by teachers and other professionals, staff training and development, parental involvement, and community inputs. In my dream school, there will be collaboration, consultation, and cooperation at all levels of educational and classroom activities.

Perspective

In my dream school, the "good school," we will move beyond tradition in the ways we identify, refer, assess, label, categorize, place, include, and instruct students. Teachers will be "good," but they will not be puritanical. They will be truly good teachers who know who they are, learn the facts when they are in doubt, change their thinking, use resource persons, build self-concepts, teach with divergent techniques, make the right choices, and continue to learn. In my dream school, a CSM that values the contributions of the self, families, schools, communities, and governments will be in operation. In other words, students will be motivated to be self-responsible, families will be empowered as they get involved, schools will shift their pedagogical paradigms, communities will be included in the educational process, and governments will provide equitable resources. Additionally, this school will be a learning community where *quality* works with a *heart*. In such a school, teachers will continue to master the craft of teaching, and the teaching-learning process will be multidimensional (Obiakor, 2000c).

My dream school will be a "good" school for the 21st century because it will maximize the fullest potential of *all* learners, *all* teachers, *all* parents, and *all* communities. In such a school, teachers will consistently be prepared to learn new ways of looking at students' experiences in their classrooms. Smith (1999) argued that teachers seem unprepared "to give thought to the way students live through a given classroom learning experience, at least in terms beyond their behavioral manifestations and test scores" (p. xxxiii). Apparently, in my dream school, students' experiences will matter, and the stories they tell will matter. Ideally, these new stories will create new directions, new hopes, new visions, new paradigms, and new traditions. In the words of Smith (1999),

Tradition has it that standardized tests, classroom performances on tests, written assignments, special projects, and cumulative grade point averages are the tools used to bracket students off as particular kinds of learners and knowledge seekers and creators . . . but such measurements of learning and knowing do not tell the complete story. Without the stories to illuminate the learning journey surrounding such measuring tools, it's not possible to fully understand if what was learned was done to satisfy oneself or someone else. Therefore, in the interest of promoting content mastery beyond a foundational level, assuming of course, that is the goal teachers wish their students to achieve, a curriculum embedded in narratives of its participants, I argue, is an invitation to discover the benefits derived from everyone's unique way of traveling through the classroom maze. (p. 153)

It seems clear to me that we cannot in good conscience continue to misidentify, misassess, mislabel, miscategorize, and misinstruct our children and youths. Phony meritocracy is counterproductive. We must believe that *all* our students can learn and that education has the *power* to change young minds. These beliefs must foster a sense of urgency as we collaborate, consult, and cooperate with each other. We need truly "good" teachers who can maximize the fullest potential of *all* students, despite their racial, cultural, and socioeconomic backgrounds. Voices of *all* learners, *all* parents, and *all* community members must remain visible as we shift our paradigms and powers in school programs. It is important that our schools solve *old* problems and create *new* solutions. Traditional presumptions have led to illusory conclusions—we can no longer afford to assume that students are "good" because they score high on standardized tests or come from *rich* homes and neighborhoods. Additionally, we can no longer afford to assume that teachers are "good" because they have been teaching for a long time or because they teach in schools located in *rich* neighborhoods. In a similar fashion, we can no longer afford to assume that schools are good because their students come from *rich* homes or because they are located in *rich* neighborhoods.

Throughout this book, my goal has been simple—*to improve cultural valuing in today's classrooms.* I have done this by challenging many retrogressive educational assumptions. I have not been interested in playing the "Black and White" political game because it dumbs down the intensity of our obligations as educators. From my perspective, no school is "good" if it discriminates against any student, whether he or she is Anglo American, African American, Hispanic American, Asian American, or Native American. The fact remains that our current educational system is Eurocentrically based. I believe we must infuse other cultural ways of thinking without denigrating those Eurocentric ways that have proved to be productive if we are going to reach *all* learners. Throughout this book, I have made it clear that "good" teachers do not misidentify, misassess, mislabel, miscategorize, and misinstruct students. Additionally, I have indicated that no student should be excluded from any "good" program. I have been blunt about this proposition. However, one of the problems in dealing with *equality* has been the argument of reverse discrimination. Although I do not believe (and have never believed) in some affirmative action or "quota" practices, many "good" educational programs that could equalize inequities seem to be eliminated today. My hunch is that "if we do not pay now, we will pay later."

Finally, it is important to realize that there is no magic standardized test—most standardized tests are biased culturally and socioeconomically. Assessments should never (I mean never) be divorced form intervention and instruction. "Good" teaching is painstaking. Just because teachers are busy does not in any way justify misidentification, misassessment, miscategorization, and misinstruction of students. This book provides multidimensional functional behavior assessment/accountability and intervention strategies. For purposes of integrity and credibility, I have referenced or quoted other pertinent sources throughout this book—my views have been buttressed by other works. The cases in this book might appear frivolous or even far-fetched, but they are very *real* experiences of *real* people. They directly attack traditional educational questions such as "Who is a 'good' student?" "Who is a 'good' teacher?" "What makes a 'good' school?" and "What makes goodness 'good?'" I believe that truly "good" teachers take risks by getting out of their comfort zones. *Quality* and *equity* must go hand in glove—they must be mutually inclusive. It is on the bases of quality and equity that I have prescribed the CSM, which takes advantage of strengths and energies of students, families, schools, communities, and governments. These entities must be empowered to work together to make a truly "good" school, our *dream school.* Ideally, we *all* can make this dream a reality.

Afterword

S chools have a lot in common with clothes, food, wine, and even beauty—everyone wants them to be "good," but there is no standard that satisfies everyone. The current push for excellence in education along with the strong press for accountability (and the consequences for children) have reinforced the critical need to define "goodness" with respect to schools and education, yet there are many competing visions of what *excellence* and *goodness* mean. At different times and in different contexts, one hears words as varied as *effective, efficient, productive,* and *high-scoring* reflecting something of a business orientation to schooling. At other times, one hears words such as *welcoming, sensitivity, comfortable,* and *nurturing,* which clearly reflect a different orientation. Plainly, there are conflicting images of what excellence entails and how one might assess it.

A strong focus in much of the school reform debate is overwhelmingly cognitive in nature. Cognitive learning outcomes are often proposed and indexed in relatively narrow ways, often as a single standardized test score. The value of the current book is that it raises these questions: What is the purpose of school? Are children more than cognitive beings? What is the responsibility of schools to promote the development of the entire child?

As Obiakor points out in this book, it is relatively easy to teach high-achieving students who are well nourished, have extensive stores of background knowledge compatible with that emphasized in school, and share many characteristics (including language or dialect) with the teacher. It is much more difficult when these conditions are not present, as often happens in large urban school districts. What we do know is that simply matching children and teachers by ethnic background is not sufficient. Obiakor convincingly argues that simple strategies are not likely to work because the problems are not simple but complex. However, he offers many ideas for what one might consider in addressing these complex issues. First and foremost, he emphasizes that learning is social first—it occurs through social relationships. As relationships go, so goes learning! The example of the Peace Corps volunteer (see pp. 111-113) is a perfect example of his point—until social relationships were cemented, no mutual exchange of learning could happen. This point is also nicely illustrated by the example of the teacher who would ignore the fact that a student's cat had died the previous day in assessing the student's poor performance. Often we need to attend to "dead cats" in order to promote learning, even though it may seem like wasted time to an outsider. Some schools and some children have more "dead cats" to attend to, and the good teacher knows when such attention is merited.

In formulating his definition of a good school, Obiakor is really talking about the principle of *responsivity* from the Vygotskian and sociocultural literature on teaching and learning. Responsivity requires a more competent or knowledgeable person to assist the learning of a less knowledgeable person by constantly monitoring learning and asking "What kind of assistance do I need to provide to get the learner to the next level of understanding?" Obiakor, throughout this book, gets at this question by using cases to specify what a good teacher in a good school might do to achieve this objective. The cases that he draws on are an excellent way of making human and real the complex reform issues that are often cast in such a technical light. They are also powerful reminders of the ways that not thinking about diversity has real consequences in the lives of students in their day-to-day school routines.

Obiakor has added a much-needed voice to the debate about excellence in education. It is a voice that adds an important aspect of balance to the discussions, which often seem to forget the students. In short, he has made a powerful argument that "cats" and other human properties have everything to do with instruction. This is a great book for all educators!

ROBERT RUEDA, PH.D.
University of Southern California

References

Algozzine, B. (1993). *50 simple ways to make teaching more fun.* Longmont, CO: Sopris West.

Anastasi, A. (1976). *Psychological testing* (4th ed.). New York: Macmillan.

Artiles, A. J. (1998). The dilemma of difference: Enriching the disproportionality discourse with theory and context. *Journal of Special Education, 32,* 32-36.

Artiles, A. J., & Trent, S. C. (1994). Overrepresentation of minority students in special education: A continual debate. *Journal of Special Education, 27,* 410-437.

Baer, G. L. (1991). *Turning our at-risk kids around.* Moravia, NY: Chronicle Guidance Publications.

Banks, J. (1999). *An introduction to multicultural education* (2nd ed.). Boston: Allyn & Bacon.

Beattie, W. R. (1982). *A treasury of business beatitudes.* New York: Doubleday.

Bessent-Byrd, H. (1995). Curricular and pedagogical procedures for African American learners with academic and cognitive disabilities. In B. A. Ford, F. E. Obiakor, & J. M. Patton (Eds.), *Effective education of African American exceptional learners: New perspectives* (pp. 123-150). Austin, TX: Pro-Ed.

Blackhurst, A. E., & Berdine, W. H. (1993). *An introduction to special education* (3rd ed.). New York: HarperCollins.

Bliss, J. R., Firestone, W. A., & Richards, C. E. (1991). *Rethinking effective schools: Research and practice.* Englewood Cliffs, NJ: Prentice Hall.

Colbert, J. A., Trimble, K., & Desberg, P. (1996). *The case for education: Contemporary approaches for using case methods.* Boston: Allyn & Bacon.

Comer, J. P., & Poussaint, A. F. (2000). Foreword. In V. G. Paley (Ed.), *White teacher* (pp. vii-xi). Cambridge, MA: Harvard University Press.

Correa, V., & Tulbert, B. (1991). Teaching culturally diverse students. *Preventing School Failure, 35,* 20-25.

DeBruyn, R. L. (1984). Upholding the tenets of education. *The Master Teacher, 15,* 1.

Denzin, N. K. (1995). The experiential text and the limits of visual understanding. *Educational Theory, 45,* 7-18.

Dewey, J. (1958). *Philosophy of education.* Ames, IA: Littlefield, Adams.

Dewey, J. (1960). *On experience, nature, and freedom.* Indianapolis, IN: Bobbs-Merrill.

Duvall, L. (1994). *Respecting our differences: A guide to getting along in a changing world.* Minneapolis, MN: Free Spirit.

Elksnin, L. K., Larsen, S. C., & Wallace, G. (1992). *Educational assessment of learning problems: Testing for teaching* (2nd ed.). Boston: Allyn & Bacon.

Ellison, R. (1972). *Invisible man.* New York: Vintage Books.

Featherstone, J. (1988). Foreword. In H. Kohl (Ed.), *Growing minds: On becoming a teacher* (pp. ix-xviii). New York: Harper Touchbooks.

Ford, B. A., Obiakor, F. E., & Patton, J. M. (Eds.) (1995). *Effective education of African American exceptional learners: New perspectives.* Austin, TX: Pro-Ed.

Ford, D. Y. (1998). The underrepresentation of minority students in gifted education: Problems and promises in recruitment and retention. *Journal of Special Education, 32,* 4-14.

Gardner, H. (1993). *Multiple intelligences: The theory of practice.* New York: Basic Books.

Gay, G. (1992). Effective teaching practices for multicultural classrooms. In C. Diaz (Ed.), *Multicultural education for the 21st century* (pp. 38-56). Washington, DC: National Education Association.

Glasser, W. (1986). *Control theory in the classroom.* New York: Harper & Row.

Goodlad, J. I. (1993). Access to knowledge. In J. I. Goodlad & T. C. Lovitt (Eds.), *Integrating general and special education* (pp. 1-22). New York: Merrill.

Gould, S. J. (1981). *The mismeasure of man.* New York: Norton.

Grilliot, L. (1995, May). *Assessment in the inclusive classroom.* Paper presented at the Great Plains Student Psychology Convention, Emporia State University, Emporia, KS.

Grossman, H. (1995). *Teaching in a diverse society.* Needham Heights, MA: Allyn & Bacon.

Grossman, H. (1998). *Ending discrimination in special education.* Springfield, IL: Charles C Thomas.

Guillaume, A. M., Zuniga-Hill, C., & Yee, I. (1995). Prospective teachers' use of diversity issues in a case study analysis. *Journal of Research and Development in Education, 28,* 69-78.

Hall, M. S. (1999). *Creative resources for the anti-bias classroom.* Albany, NY: Dalmar.

Halvorsen, A. T., & Neary, T. (2001). *Building inclusive schools: Tools and strategies for success.* Boston: Allyn & Bacon.

Harris-Obiakor, P. (2000, June). *Communicating effectively in the workplace.* Paper presented at the Student Technological Conference, University of Wisconsin–Milwaukee.

Henderson, G., & Bibens, R. F. (1970). *Teachers should care: Social perspectives of teaching.* New York: Harper & Row.

Herrnstein, R. J. (1971, September). I.Q. *Atlantic Monthly,* pp. 43-64.

Herrnstein, R. J., & Murray, C. (1994). *The bell curve: Intelligence and class structure in American life.* New York: Free Press.

Hilliard, A. G. (1992). The pitfalls and promises of special education practice. *Exceptional Children, 59,* 168-172.

Hilliard, A. G. (1995). Culture, assessment, and valid teaching for the African American student. In B. A. Ford, F. E. Obiakor, & J. M. Patton (Eds.), *Effective education of African American exceptional learners: New perspectives* (pp. ix-xvi). Austin, TX: Pro-Ed.

Hobbs, N. (1975). *The futures of children: Categories, labels, and their consequences.* San Francisco: Jossey-Bass.

Hoyle, E. (1975). *The role of the teacher.* London: Routledge & Kegan Paul.

Jensen, A. (1973). The differences are real. *Psychology Today, 7,* 80-86.

Jensen, A. (1985). Compensatory education and the theory of intelligence. *Phi Delta Kappan, 66,* 559-564.

Johnson, E. W. (1981). *Teaching school: Points picked up.* New York: Walker.

Karr, S., & Wright, J. (1995). Assessment: Proper use for persons with problem behaviors. In F. E. Obiakor & B. Algozzine (Eds.), *Managing problem behaviors: Perspectives for general and special educators* (pp. 63-95). Dubuque, IA: Kendall/Hunt.

Kauffman, J. M. (1989). *Characteristics of behavior disorders of children and youth* (4th ed.). Columbus, OH: Merrill.

Kauffman, J. M., & Ford, D. Y. (1998). Introduction to the special section. *Journal of Special Education, 32,* 3.

Kauffman, J. M., & Hallahan, D. P. (1995). *The illusion of full inclusion: A comprehensive critique of a current special education bandwagon.* Austin, TX: Pro-Ed.

Kea, C. D., & Utley, C. A. (1998). To teach me is to know me. *Journal of Special Education, 32,* 44-51.

King, C. S. (1983). *The words of Martin Luther King, Jr.* New York: Newmarket Press.

Kohl, H. (1988). *Growing minds: On becoming a teacher.* New York: Harper Touchbooks.

Ladson-Billings, G. (1994). *The dreamkeepers: Successful teachers of African American children.* San Francisco: Jossey-Bass.

Ladson-Billings, G. (2000). Teaching in dangerous times. *Rethinking Schools: An Urban Education Journal, 14,* 1, 18-19.

Lovitt, T. (1977). *In spite of my resistance... I've learned from children.* Columbus, OH: Merrill.

Lovitt, T. (2000). *Preventing school failure: Tactics for teaching adolescents* (2nd ed.). Austin, TX: Pro-Ed.

McConnell, M. E., Hilvitz, P. B., & Cox, C. J. (1998). Functional assessment: A systematic process for assessment and intervention in general and special education classrooms. *Intervention in School and Clinic, 34,* 10-20.

Mercer, J. R. (1972). IQ: The lethal label. *Psychology Today, 6,* 44-47, 95-97.

Mercer, J. R. (1973). *Labeling the mentally retarded: Clinical and social system perspectives on mental retardation.* Berkeley: University of California Press.

Mickler, M. J. (1994). Academic self-concept: An exploration of traditions. In F. E. Obiakor & S. W. Stile (Eds.), *Self-concepts of exceptional learners: Current perspectives for educators* (Rev. ed., pp. 121-155). Dubuque, IA: Kendall/Hunt.

Midgette, J. E. (1995). Assessment of African American exceptional learners: New strategies and perspectives. In B. A. Ford, F. E. Obiakor, & J. M. Patton (Eds.), *Effective education of African American exceptional learners: New perspectives* (pp. 3-25). Austin, TX: Pro-Ed.

Milwaukee Catalyst. (1998). *Facts: A resource guide.* Milwaukee, WI: Author.

National Institute for Urban School Improvement. (2000). *Improving education: The promise of inclusive schools* [On-line]. Available: http://www.edc.org/urban/Inclbook.htm

Obiakor, F. E. (1992, October/November). Self-concept of African American students: An operational model for special education. *Exceptional Education, 59,* 160-167.

Obiakor, F. E. (1994). *The eight-step multicultural approach: Learning and teaching with a smile.* Dubuque, IA: Kendall/Hunt.

Obiakor, F. E. (1996a). Collaboration, consultation, and cooperation: The "whole village at work." In N. Gregg, R. C. Curtis, & S. F. Schmidt (Eds.), *African American adolescents and adults: An overview of assessment issues* (pp. 77-91). Athens: University of Georgia/Roosevelt Warm Springs Institute for Rehabilitation, Learning Disabilities Research and Training Center.

Obiakor, F. E. (1996b, January 24). The power of the word. *Emporia Gazette,* p. 7.

Obiakor, F. E. (1999a). *Beyond the steps: Multicultural study guide.* Dubuque, IA: Kendall/Hunt.

Obiakor, F. E. (1999b). Multicultural education: Powerful tool for educating learners with exceptionalities. In F. E. Obiakor, J. O. Schwenn, & A. F. Rotatori (Eds.), *Advances in education:*

Multicultural education for learners with exceptionalities (pp. 1-14). Stamford, CT: JAI.

Obiakor, F. E. (1999c). Teacher expectations of minority exceptional learners: Impact on "accuracy" of self-concepts. *Exceptional Children, 66,* 39-53.

Obiakor, F. E. (2000a, April). *Infusing multicultural models in teacher education program: Vision for the new millennium.* Paper presented at the International Convention of the Council for Exceptional Children, Vancouver, BC, Canada.

Obiakor, F. E. (2000b, July). *Redefining "good" schools: Quality and equity in education.* Position paper #1 presented as Distinguished Visiting Professor, West Virginia University, Morgantown, WV.

Obiakor, F. E. (2000c, October). *Transforming teaching-learning to improve student achievement.* Position paper at the Best Practice Conference, Institute for the Transformation of Learning, Marquette University, Milwaukee, WI.

Obiakor, F. E., & Algozzine, B. (1995). *Managing problem behaviors: Perspectives for general and special education.* Dubuque, IA: Kendall/Hunt.

Obiakor, F. E., Darling, S., & Ford, B. A. (2000, April). *Managing crises of suburban students: What general and special educators must know.* Program Chair Invited Session presented at the International Convention of the Council for Exceptional Children, Vancouver, BC, Canada.

Obiakor, F. E., Harris-Obiakor, P., Obi, S. O., & Eskay, M. (2000). Urban learners in general and special education programs: Revisiting assessment and intervention issues. In F. E. Obiakor, S. A. Burkhardt, A. F. Rotatori, & T. Wahlberg (Eds.), *Advances in education: Intervention techniques for individuals with exceptionalities in inclusive settings* (pp. 115-131). Stamford, CT: JAI.

Obiakor, F. E., Karr, S., Utley, C., & Algozzine, B. (1998). The requirements and demands of being an educator. In R. J. Anderson, C. E. Keller, & J. M. Karp (Eds.), *Enhancing diversity: Educators with disabilities* (pp. 142-154). Washington, DC: Gallaudet University Press.

Obiakor, F. E., Mehring, T. A., & Schwenn, J. O. (1997). *Disruption, disaster, and death: Helping students deal with crises.* Reston, VA: Council for Exceptional Children.

Obiakor, F. E., & Schwenn, J. O. (1995). Enhancing self-concepts of culturally diverse students: The role of the counselor. In A. F. Rotatori, J. O. Schwenn, & F. W. Litton (Eds.), *Advances in special education: Counseling special populations. Research and practice perspectives* (Vol. 9, pp. 191-206). Greenwich, CT: JAI.

Obiakor, F. E., & Schwenn, J. O. (1996). Assessment of culturally diverse students with behavior disorders. In A. F. Rotatori, J. O. Schwenn, & S. Burkhardt (Eds.), *Advances in special education: Assessment and psychopathology issues in special education* (Vol. 10, pp. 37-57). Greenwich, CT: JAI.

Obiakor, F. E., Schwenn, J. O., & Rotatori, A. F. (Eds.) (1999). *Advances in special education: Multicultural education for learners with exceptionalities.* Stamford, CT: JAI.

Obiakor, F. E., & Utley, C. A. (1997). Rethinking preservice preparation for teachers in the learning disabilities field: Workable multicultural strategies. *Learning Disabilities Research and Practice, 12,* 100-106.

Obiakor, F. E., & Williams, D. (2000, March). *Using cases to infuse multicultural models in teacher preparation programs: Vision for the new millennium.* Paper presented at the 12th Annual School of Education Research Conference, University of Wisconsin–Milwaukee.

O'Brien, S. J. (1991, Spring). How do you raise respectful children in a disrespectful world? *Childhood Education,* pp. 183-184.

Orlich, D. C., Harder, R. J., Callahan, R. C., & Gibson, H. W. (2001). *Teaching strategies: A guide to better instruction* (6th ed.). Boston: Houghton Mifflin.

Paley, V. G. (2000). *White teacher.* Cambridge, MA: Harvard University Press.

Palmer, P. J. (1998). *The courage to teach: Exploring the inner landscape of a teacher's life.* San Francisco: Jossey-Bass.

Park, E. K., Pullis, M., Reilly, T. F., & Townsend, B. L. (1994). Cultural bias in the identification of students with behavior disorders. In R. L. Peterson & S. Ishii-Jordan (Eds.), *Multi-*

cultural issues in the education of students with behavior disorders (pp. 14-26). Cambridge, MA: Brookline.

Patton, J. M. (1998). The disproportionate representation of African Americans in special education: Looking behind the curtain for understanding and solutions. *Journal of Special Education, 32,* 25-31.

Peterson, R. (1992). *Life in a crowded place: Making a learning community.* Portsmouth, NH: Heinemann.

Pool, H., & Page, J. A. (1995). *Beyond tracking: Finding success in inclusive schools.* Bloomington, IN: Phi Delta Kappa Educational Foundation.

Proctor, C. P. (1984). Teacher expectations: A model for school improvement. *Elementary School Journal, 84,* 121-130.

Redl, F., & Wattenberg, W. (1951). *Mental hygiene in teaching.* New York: Harcourt Brace.

Rogers, H. C. (1984). *Rogers' rules for success.* New York: St. Martin's/Marek.

Rosenthal, R., & Jacobson, L. (1968). *Pygmalion in the classroom.* New York: Holt, Rinehart & Winston.

Rotatori, A. F., & Obi, S. O. (1999). Directions for the future: Empowering the culturally diverse exceptional learners. In F. E. Obiakor, J. O. Schwenn, & A. F. Rotatori (Eds.), *Advances in special education: Multicultural education for learners with exceptionalities* (pp. 233-242). Stamford, CT: JAI.

Salvia, J., & Ysseldyke, J. E. (1981). *Assessment in special and remedial education* (2nd ed.). Boston: Houghton Mifflin.

School District of Shorewood, Wisconsin. (1997). *Shorewood's gifted and talented education.* Shorewood, WI: Author.

Smith, D. D. (1998). *Introduction to special education: Teaching in an age of challenge* (3rd ed.). Needham Heights, MA: Allyn & Bacon.

Smith, D. J. (1999). *Stepping inside the classroom through personal narratives.* Lanham, MD: University Press of America.

Toffler, A. (1982). *The third wave.* New York: Bantam.

Trent, S. C., Obiakor, F. E., Ford, B. A., & Artiles, A. J. (2000, April). *Educating minority exceptional learners in the new millennium.* Preconvention workshop presented at the International Convention of the Council for Exceptional Children, Vancouver, BC, Canada.

Trotter, T. V. (1993). Counseling with young multicultural clients. In A. Vernon (Ed.), *Counseling children and adolescents* (pp. 137-155). Denver, CO: Love.

Utley, C. A., Delquadri, J. C., Obiakor, F. E., & Mims, V. (2000). General and special educators' perceptions of teaching strategies for culturally and linguistically diverse students. *Teacher Education and Special Education, 23,* 34-50.

Valles, E. C. (1998). The disproportionate representation of minority students in special education: Responding to the problem. *Journal of Special Education, 32,* 52-54.

Weaver, K. (1994, March). *Experiences of a peacecorper.* Emporia, KS: Emporia State University.

Wechsler, D. (1991). *Manual for the Wechsler Intelligence Scale for Children–Third Edition.* San Antonio, TX: Psychological Corporation.

West, C. (1993). *Race matters.* New York: Vintage.

Westby, C. E., & Rouse, G. R. (1985). Culture in education and the instruction of language in learning disabled students. *Topics in Language Disorders, 5,* 15-28.

Wisconsin Department of Public Instruction. (2000). *Information update: Least restrictive environment.* Madison, WI: Author.

Witt, J. C., Elliot, S. M., Kraub, J. J., & Gresham, F. M. (1994). *Assessment of children: Fundamental methods and practices.* Madison, WI: Brown & Benchmark.

Ysseldyke, J. E., Algozzine, B., & Thurlow, M. L. (2000). *Critical issues in special education* (3rd ed.). Boston: Houghton Mifflin.

Index